W9-CYD-383

Igniting
Customer Connections

Igniting
Customer Connections

FIRE UP YOUR COMPANY'S GROWTH BY MULTIPLYING
CUSTOMER EXPERIENCE & ENGAGEMENT

ANDY FRAWLEY

WILEY

Library of Congress Cataloging-in-Publication Data:

Frawley, Andy.
    Igniting customer connections : fire up your company's growth by multiplying customer experience & engagement / Andrew Frawley.
        pages cm
    Includes index.
        ISBN 978-1-118-91670-4 (hardback); ISBN 978-1-118-91671-1 (ebk);
ISBN 978-1-118-91672-8 (ebk)
    1. Customer relations.   2. Marketing.   3. Customer loyalty.   I. Title.
    HF5415.5.F72 2014
    658.8'12–dc23

2014025630

CONTENTS

PREFACE

Marketing Is on Fire

Are You Basking in the Warm Glow or Getting Burned?

You are a marketer. So am I. And I've been one for more than 30 years, giving me a unique perspective on our business and the marketplace. This book, however, is not an anecdote-filled memoir, because the old ways of marketing are over, and I'm not interested in revisiting them. I'm much more fascinated by what's happening now—and excited about helping our industry rethink some of its core tenets. I want to help marketers be more effective, drive profitability, and earn new respect within their organizations. And I want to help solve the number-one challenge that every marketer faces in our chaotic, lightning-fast marketplace—how to deploy your marketing resources to create an emotional connection with customers and engage them in new, effective ways that achieve impressive, repeatable results.

During the past few years I have seen clients fundamentally change the performance of their marketing by simultaneously focusing their strategies on improving how customers *engage* with their brand and how they (and the broader base of consumers) *experience* the brand. They're not just observing this connection. They're proactively allocating marketing strategies and dollars to improve engagement and experience, and are ultimately improving business outcomes—including sales, share of wallet, and brand equity—dramatically.

That said, I wanted to write a book not based on theory or simple anecdotal examples. So I have commissioned proprietary research that provides clear insight and direction in terms of how we, as marketers, should optimize the range of diverse new channels, media, and technologies to drive brand and business equity.

I'll be introducing you to an innovative new way of inspiring and measuring major leaps in customer experience and engagement. We call it **Return on Experience × Engagement**, or **ROE^2**. It may look like a simple mathematical expression, but it's a powerful tool for marketers, with major implications for business outcomes such as brand and business equity. In the research section of this book (Part Two), you will see impressive results that show the power of ROE^2—such as the ability to *triple* brand and business equity by addressing experience and engagement together.

In short, this book does more than just describe ROE^2. It delivers data that proves its efficacy. And it includes first-person accounts from leaders at organizations that are using it to increase customer engagement and drive profitability.

Ultimately, ROE^2 is a commonsense approach that you as a marketing professional need to have at your fingertips—no matter how large your organization or what you're marketing.

Meet the Powerful Combination of Engagement
and Experience—ROE^2

In this book, we'll explore a refreshingly effective approach that helps you drive more profitable customer connections and measure the impact of your marketing—Return on Experience × Engagement, or ROE^2. At its essence, ROE^2 looks at the ways that marketers can drive engagement and experience *together* in a way that creates a dramatic impact on business outcomes, such as brand equity, share of wallet, and lifetime value.

- **Part One** explains the approach, why it's so different, and how it can complement return on investment (ROI), the standard but outmoded way of evaluating marketing.

- **Part Two** shows how it works via research especially commissioned for this book—plus interviews with executives with firsthand insights on ROE^2. Here we will break down the individual components of engagement and experience and look at the predictive powers for improving your business.

- **Part Three** dives more deeply into the fundamental elements of ROE^2—content, channels, measurement/segmentation, and technology (in all its many permutations)—providing a clear primer for marketers who want all the details on how to make ROE^2 happen. This section concludes with an overview of consumer privacy issues, a key area that every marketer needs to be conversant in.

Let me give you a simple, single-channel example of Experience $\times$ Engagement and why a new metric like ROE^2 is so important. I have the privilege and opportunity to work with some of the most sophisticated retail and e-commerce e-mail marketers in the world. During the holiday season, many will e-mail their customers daily or multiple times a day. This approach often drives *engagement* in the form of opens and clicks that lead to short-term sales. However, over the past few years we have seen that opt-out rates increase as well during this period. Research has shown that consumers don't like the *experience* with a brand that is filling up their mailbox. So what is the trade-off—do you make a short-term sale but lose a customer forever?

ROE^2 excels in these situations by providing a framework, and even an equation, to help marketers make these hard decisions.

A Quick Look at the Past

To get started, let's take a brief glance in the rearview mirror. When I started in marketing, the channels (TV, radio, mail, telemarketing) and types of campaigns were limited and the pace was slow. A direct marketing campaign generally meant direct mail or telemarketing. It might take three or four months for a campaign to go from ideation to execution. The job of the marketer was to run a few major campaigns every year. Success meant people expressing increased brand awareness, people carrying fliers into stores, bringing a friend with them, or calling a catalog order center. It was all one-way communication. We controlled the content, timing, and cadence of the messages—and the messages were inherently limited.

Campaigns might have a couple of versions. They were launched every quarter or every year and evaluated strictly on the sales that could be directly attributed to them in a single channel. Brands could only learn about customers and their preferences three or four times a year, if they were lucky. We relied exclusively on market research to understand people's attitudes. There was no way to interact individually with customers at a large-scale level. It was simply too complicated and expensive.

Now, Everything Has Changed—for the Better

Major shifts in consumer behavior and the advent of powerful (and affordable) new marketing tools are driving a quantum leap in marketing sophistication, effectiveness, and complexity. Today's marketers have an unprecedented opportunity to combine the best of both disciplines—the reach of mass marketing and the targeting of direct marketing—opening up powerful new approaches to drive engagement and experience.

Consider these facts about consumer behavior. There are more smartphones than people on our planet. Since consumers are totally mobile, channel distinctions don't matter as much as they used to—decisions are made on the spot, 24/7, at home, on the road, and in stores. The path to a buying decision may include a digital ad, an online search, a smartphone price check, and advice gathered via social media. In fact, more than 58 percent of U.S. smartphone and tablet owners are using their mobile devices to learn about products or prices—either online or while in a physical store, according to research from the website testing and personalization firm Maxymiser. Social networks have a huge influence on purchasing behavior as consumers take more control. And that's just one side of the story.

On the marketing side, incredible new tools are available, and digital marketing spending is skyrocketing. Major players like Adobe, Salesforce.com, IBM, and Oracle are investing heavily in the marketing space, as traditional technology companies see the value of marketing and the impact that technology can play. Savvy marketers and the brands they work for are already beginning to take advantage of these incredible technologies and designing new tools, strategies, and techniques to make new inroads into the changing marketplace. They are working to take advantage of the unbelievable array of opportunities created by fast-paced, multichannel marketing. Content can be more relevant, personalized, and consistent. Campaign cycle times are measured in minutes rather than days. After all, marketers can reach millions of potential customers with a single click, e-mail, post, or tweet. Ultimately, new customer insights are triggering new transformations as organizations rethink their core processes and align them around customer-centric delivery.

It All Starts with Customer Connections

The ability to conduct dozens of targeted campaigns, to gather detailed customer data, and then to use it to generate impressive results—these possibilities make marketing exhilarating. Never before have marketers had the opportunity to drive such dramatic improvements in their business—engaging new consumers, expanding their customer bases, boosting revenues, and building their brands. Consider these recent results:

- **A major consumer packaged goods (CPG) brand** generated one billion impressions via the use of emotionally engaging, multichannel, user-generated content.

- **A large bank** reduced customer attrition by 20 percent by triggering client-specific content based on account engagement.

- **An e-commerce site** increased its conversion rates on e-mail by 15 percent by doing device detection and retargeting e-mails based on whether recipients opened e-mails on their computers or on their smartphones.

These impressive results aren't enabled by technological advances alone. They happened because marketers took full advantage of the capabilities available to them, injected great content, and nimbly avoided the downside. Understanding and balancing these two elements—the potential and the pitfalls—will determine the winners and losers. To succeed during a time of new challenges and great potential rewards, marketers must master the power of the new technologies and channels, while finding new ways to use data and rich media content to drive the emotional connection to a brand, the end goal that has defined marketing success for generations. To do that requires a new approach to customer connections and a new way to determine success—ROE^2.

For Marketers of All Stripes and Types

I wrote *Igniting Customer Connections* to help marketers like you use data, content, and technology to forge customer connections in ways that were unthinkable just a few years ago. This book is intended to help you take advantage of the amazing capabilities available today—and also get the respect (and promotion, of course) that hard-working marketers deserve. It provides a unique set of research and intellectual property designed to guide you to the next generation of successful marketing—turning marketing from a cost center to a vital function that systematically drives profitability for your organization.

Start the Fire—Now

Igniting customer connections starts with a single spark—a new idea, a revolutionary approach, or advice that makes a real difference. I think ROE^2 is that spark, and I'm very excited to pass it on to you. Let's begin.

Part One
Connect with Your Customers—*Now*

Chapter 1
The New Marketing Landscape

To Survive Here, You Need to Be Able to Deal with Complexity and Speed

Marketing successfully to an ever-shifting audience is always challenging, but even more so in a time of more *and* less. We have more channels for connecting with people, dozens of customer touch points, mountains of consumer data, and a global reach. But we also have closer scrutiny of marketing spend, a focus on consumer privacy, and less time to make critical decisions and deliver a message to a much more empowered (and possibly jaded) audience. In an era of Big Data and advanced analytics, of multiple screens and marketing-intolerant customers who can shut them off, what's the best path ahead? And how do we know what factors are creating customer engagement and driving profitability—not just today, but over time?

Let's start by taking a look at the megatrends or *tectonic shifts* that have changed the way we produce and access information. Then we'll explore how these shifts have changed the way consumers behave.

Tectonic Shift #1: More Media, Devices, and Disruption

For years, access to media meant TV, radio, billboards, and other content produced by large, centralized entities sending down content from the upper echelons of advertising, marketing, and communication. Now media is in the palm of every consumer's hand, and everyone is a producer. Smartphones, tablets, and more devices have enabled a major disruption in the flow of information, moving it from *broadcast* and *controlled* to free-form, decentralized content created by almost anyone. The proliferation and fragmentation of channels have led to shorter attention spans and less time spent by the consumer in any one channel. (See Figure 1.1.) Accordingly, spending has shifted (and continues to shift) from concentrated mass media to more data-driven, direct, primarily digital channels.

Tectonic Shift #2: The Data Deluge

More and more media is digital, meaning that media and channels are generating and consuming massive amounts of data, leading to the proverbial *data deluge*. Data is now available everywhere, on almost every topic—and individual consumer. Digital channels not only allow instantaneous connections but also generate huge amounts of data about a consumer's activities and interests. In fact, one week of web behavioral data is equal in size to an entire marketing database's volume 10 years ago.

This data is shifting from controlled and regulated to decentralized and self-curated. So user-generated content, such as a crucial tweet, can move faster than the traditional powers—government and private industry. For example, when American Apparel tweeted its ill-considered "Hurricane Sandy Sale" in 2012, consumers took to the Twittersphere and created their own storm of disapproval. In just one day, the sentiment score for the company decreased by 60 points, according to *AdWeek*.

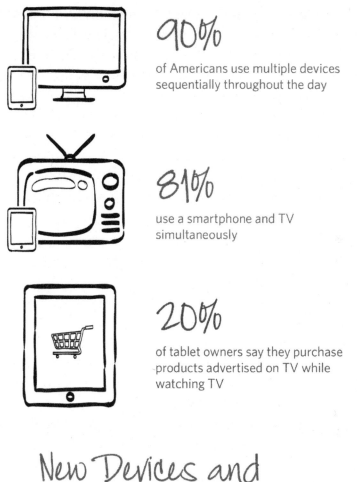

90%
of Americans use multiple devices sequentially throughout the day

81%
use a smartphone and TV simultaneously

20%
of tablet owners say they purchase products advertised on TV while watching TV

New Devices and Ways to Use Them

Figure 1.1   These statistics from Nielsen and Statista show that consumers are changing the way they use their multiple devices to interact with brands.

Tectonic Shift #3: The Infrastructure Goes Global

The marketing landscape used to seem narrow and fairly defined for all but the biggest brands. Now expanding digital channels extend that landscape significantly. The focus can be global for brands that want to be global, and local for those that want to stay that way. The Internet (and especially mobile) knows no geographic bounds. You can reach customers in Hong Kong as well as those around the corner, if you choose to take that route and invest the money to do it right. You can tailor your message to their culture and language. And you can distribute your product with remarkable efficiency—or fail by thinking it's easy and disappointing your customers (and triggering ripples of wider consumer disappointment). The challenge for many organizations would be unimaginable a decade ago—taking full advantage of globally distributed transactions while providing localized support.

Tectonic Shift #4: Digital Channels Create Opportunities for Companies of All Sizes

Sophisticated multichannel marketing used to be the domain of only the largest companies with big marketing departments and complex technologies. Today, mobile and social media are great normalizers and equalizers. Anyone can have a Facebook page and a Twitter feed. They can quickly populate it with content—and customers can help. A small or emerging business can have global reach instantly, and at a very low cost.

Tectonic Shift #5: The World Moves Faster Than Ever

Traditional marketing—and by that I mean marketing from a decade ago or even less—looks really slow from our current vantage point, while the landscape looks far bigger (and harder to traverse) than in the past. Now that traditional marketing has shifted to digital media, now that marketers are interactive marketers, now that consumers are *always on*, the speed of change is faster than ever—for customers and the brands that serve them. Brands have the unequaled opportunity to be connected in real time to customers, as well as the challenge of delivering a unified customer experience in a multichannel world. Consumers expect a lightning-fast response from their brands—to a request, complaint, or review. They want respectful, responsive service. In fact, 71 percent of consumers agree: valuing their time is the most important factor in good customer service. And the stakes are higher, since one customer's dissatisfaction can quickly spread. But get it right, and consumers spread that news as well.

No one has enough time, creating a degree of time starvation that is reflected in all aspects of consumer behavior. For marketers, this lack of time means that you must be agile, delivering information designed to be consumed and understood quickly. And dynamic content generation speeds the whole process even more.

Tectonic Shifts Drive Crucial Changes in Consumer Behavior

What have these tectonic shifts done to affect the way consumers behave? Plenty.

- **Consumers are never more than an arm's length from all the information in the world.** They can communicate with each other (and brands), engage in social media, and conduct research on products and much more—anytime, anywhere. And *always on* means being in a shopping state of mind. On average, 73 percent of participants in a recent study visited a retail location after receiving a location-aware text message. And 61 percent made a purchase as a result of the message, according to eMarketer and Forrester Research.

- **Consumers are connected to each other in new ways.** The news (good or bad) spreads faster than ever. People talk, tweet, post, and blog. And their reach is just as broad as ours as marketers. Every citizen-buyer is a marketer now, just like everyone is an

Figure 1.2 Millennial consumers are more likely to trust their peers than brands, with 50 percent reading reviews on their mobile devices while shopping (versus 21 percent of nonmillennials, according to Forrester Research).

on-the-scene reporter—whether they choose to take advantage of that role or not.

- **The purchase path is nonlinear.** Consumers are making decisions in real time, wherever they go. Customers are making buying decisions all the time—on their tablets, on their phones, or at work when they're supposed to be doing something else. The path to purchase is now less of a journey and more of a *decision space*, where consumers enter and leave based on their readiness to buy—and the ability of marketers to move them into that zone.

Marketing interactions, once quarterly or monthly, are happening all the time, and in exponential numbers. A major marketing organization may have thousands of campaigns running all the time. In fact,

The World Is Open for Business

Figure 1.3   Everywhere commerce turns shopping inside out. Purchasing can take place anywhere or any time a consumer has access to a screen. By 2017, mobile commerce will account for 26 percent of U.S. retail e-commerce sales (eMarketer).

the word *campaign*—implying a long, concerted effort—may no longer apply. It's more about marketing *interactions*—small, focused, agile efforts aimed at achieving a near-term goal while building deeper, long-term customer connections.

- **Social media has a powerful voice.** Thanks to ubiquitous social media, *global* and *local* are more intertwined than ever. The ripple effects of events happening across the world—of revolutions, extreme weather, economic trends, and more—have a local impact, good or bad. One image of your company's product or logo in the wrong place at the wrong time can undermine years of good intentions.

- **Consumers have high expectations.** Particularly among younger consumers, the expectations for content and communication are high, boosted by Amazon.com, YouTube, and much more. Consumers expect relevant recommendations at the right time. They expect consistency across all channels. And video and other rich media aren't an exception anymore. They're the standard, and that standard continues to grow. To be effective, marketing needs to be in the media vernacular of the moment, or (ideally) ahead of that moment. After all, 65 percent of your audience learns visually,

Figure 1.4   Consumers are more likely to opt in and exchange privacy for relevant messaging that they see value in. Eighty-one percent of recipients of e-mails containing personalization drawing from previous shopping behaviors and preferences are more likely to increase their purchases. Thirty-one percent are willing to share a mobile number, and 32 percent are willing to share their social handles (eMarketer, National Retail Federation).

according to WebDAM Marketing Trends for 2014. And visual data is processed 60,000 times faster by the brain than text is.

- **Information about a consumer's experience and emotion are widely available.** In the past, we had to rely on focus groups and anecdotes to understand the emotional feelings of consumers. Today, through social media, most consumers are volunteering lots of information about how they feel. This information, along with low-cost surveys, allows brands to actively use emotional data as an aspect of their audience selection and segmentation.

- **Consumers will be willing to trust you if you get it right.** If brands deliver on their promises, personalize communications, create relevant offers, and respect privacy, consumers can still express old-fashioned loyalty. It just may not last as long as it used to.

- *They* **control the message.** The balance of power has shifted from brands to consumers. And the impact of consumer empowerment cannot be underestimated. Yes, there are more and more channels and consumer touch points. But the consumer has the power to turn off, delete, and block messaging. So respecting consumers' time and intelligence is even more important than ever. Otherwise the all-important customer connection can be diminished or even lost.

What Does an Empowered Consumer Mean?

The empowerment of consumers with new, faster ways to communicate globally can be a blessing or a curse to brands. On the plus side, the world is your audience—more prospects, customers, and potential revenue. We, as marketers, are delivering programs into the marketplace that are driving tremendous results on a scale that couldn't have been achieved in the past. But consumer empowerment also means that brands have to consider the potential social impact—at all levels, from manufacturing to marketing. No apparel company wants to be the brand behind a collapsed sweatshop in Southeast Asia. No organization wants to do anything that it wouldn't want to see in its customers' Facebook Timeline or Twitter feed. No technology brand wants to send out a marketing message that manages to offend a faraway nation. All the impact comes back home now, faster than ever.

One fact is clear—the consumer is increasingly in the driver's seat. Ordinary people are seizing an extraordinary ability to change the way they communicate, buy, and live. This disrupted, consumer-driven marketplace opens up new opportunities for marketers to deliver relevant information and offers that meld seamlessly with the consumer's lifestyle. But it all starts with making stronger, deeper customer connections.

An empowered consumer creates very different marketing experiences, more complicated buying patterns, and a higher degree of uncertainty about what consumers will do. As we move into the future, "we must become more comfortable with probability and uncertainty," says Nate Silver, renowned statistician and predictor of everything from baseball to presidential elections. This insight points toward a much more fluid, ever-changing world. In that context, successful marketing needs to recognize that there's not one predefined path for every consumer. Every action triggers a reaction and multiple paths forward. Marketers need to anticipate and predict consumer needs as accurately as possible by using data, insights, and the wide array of tools now available. Only then can we ensure that marketing is relevant and effective.

Marketing Isn't a Mystery Anymore

Consumers are smarter about marketing now. Back in the day, they just passively accepted whatever came through their TVs. They didn't have a choice. It was just *there*. Now, thanks to a broader awareness of what marketing is, people know when they're being marketed to—and they have the power to block, ignore, undermine, or opt out of the deluge of messaging and media coming through all of their many screens.

After all, we live in a multiscreen world—which is great for reaching more prospects via the channels they choose. But more marketing can also mean messaging overload, customer fatigue, and diminishing returns. And the consumer holds the device—whether it's a mobile phone, a tablet, or a laptop. So consumers are in control. They will choose the channels that deliver the most relevant experience and seamless buying process, and will ignore the rest.

Meet the Me Economy

The marketing landscape used to be simple and limited. If you wanted to buy a television set, you went to an electronics store, compared models, and bought one. Now, you would probably do some online research, compare your options (Amazon vs. brick-and-mortar stores), and buy via the channel that offered the best value and experience. The purchase path may be very nonlinear and highly idiosyncratic to the individual buyer, brand, category, and product. In short, the herd mentality is over, as are the days of thinking about buying in terms of research, purchase, and loyalty. Now we're dealing with *economies of one*, the so-called *me economy*—where content is personalized for everyone, where micro-transactions happen every moment, where consumers filter messages, and where social and virtual currencies may be as important as hard cash.

What Do These Shifts and Trends Mean to You?

To be successful, marketers need to be relevant, in the moment, enabled at the transaction level, creating an emotional connection, and super-agile, so you can adapt to rise above the noise. As we'll see in the next chapters of *Igniting Customer Connections*, brands like yours need to take full advantage of the current marketing landscape, with all its megatrends and consumer behaviors, to build better business outcomes (e.g., brand and business equity) that will propel it ahead.

How? By focusing on a powerful combination of customer experience and engagement. And it all starts by creating strong *connections*, which we explore in detail in the next chapter.

Marketing Converges

For years, the worlds of direct marketing (with its disciplined focus on marketing to identified customers or prospects) and mass media (focused on broad-based exposure) existed in separate universes. Mass marketing slowly gave way to direct marketing, which offered more measurable outcomes, better targeting, and more agility. Today, they can be combined, thanks to digital channels and the ability to manage large sets of information. This convergence gives marketers new opportunities to combine the best of both disciplines—the reach of mass marketing and the targeting of direct marketing—creating innovative, powerful approaches.

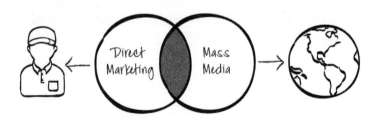

The Converging Worlds
of Marketing

The New Marketing Landscape

- The marketplace is fast, fragmented, and fueled by empowered consumers.

- Engaging with today's consumers means meeting them on their terms.

- Omnichannel consumers are the new norm.

- Consumers are fickle.

- Consumer-driven content has a major impact.

- The new marketplace demands new marketing approaches.

Chapter 2
Customer Connections

The Basic Concept Remained Unchanged for Hundreds of Years—Until Now

With the major shifts and upheaval in the marketplace and evolving consumer behavior, businesses want and need to forge strong connections with their customers—now more than ever. One of the central premises of the book is that both experience and engagement are created, amplified, or destroyed—one connection at a time. So marketers need the kind of connections that result in positive brand equity and sales, and other positive business outcomes—now and in the future. Taking your marketing to the next level means really understanding what makes up a connection and then moving higher up the hierarchy of customer connections. Here we take a look at that hierarchy and how it applies to your customers.

Connections Exist at Many Levels

In your personal life, you probably trust the people you feel highly connected with (your spouse) more than those with whom you share only a passing connection (your barista). So it goes in the marketplace, where

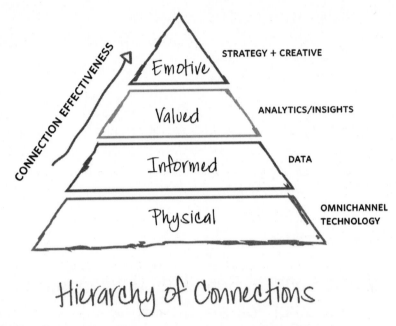

Figure 2.1   Maslow's Hierarchy of Needs puts the largest, most fundamental type of needs (breathing, food, water) at the bottom of the pyramid and the secondary, more sophisticated needs at the top. Maslow's theory suggests that the most basic levels of needs must be met before the individual can focus on the secondary needs. So it is with the Hierarchy of Connections. The basics (the bottom of the pyramid) have to be achieved to enable achievement of the higher levels.

there's a Hierarchy of Connections—a new construct we've created that builds on Abraham Maslow's Hierarchy of Needs, which you may remember from psychology class. As the customer connection becomes stronger, so does its effectiveness.

The Core Elements of a Connection

Consider that a *connection*, whether in a personal, business, or marketing context, relies on four key components:

1. The ability to communicate with a targeted individual. Connection requires communication of some type, ideally clear, direct, and reliable. Without communication, connection is impossible, of course. With omnichannel connections, the array of options expands for marketers, as does the responsibility to use these channels effectively.

2. **Accurate information about the individual.** To connect with people, you need to know who they are and something about them. If you don't know anything about them, it's going to be a one-sided conversation and the connection will be minimal. In the context of marketing, this knowledge is enabled and exponentially expanded by the wealth of first- and third-party data available to describe and define a customer.

3. **Awareness of what the individual values.** The connection builds and strengthens as you begin to know the unique values of that individual. In the marketing world, these values start to translate into how people feel. Do they value a great deal or exceptional craftsmanship? Being associated with a popular brand or a more visionary/iconoclastic brand? Paper or plastic? Organic or conventional? Every consumer is a unique collection of accumulated and ever-evolving values and choices.

4. **An emotional connection to the individual.** Emotional connection is the highest level. A shared system of beliefs, a common experience, commitment to a cause—these can all trigger a strong emotional connection. Strategic, creative marketing appeals to the emotions of consumers via images, sounds, ideas, and the ever-important *feelings*—because rationality and emotionality coexist in each of us. As you'll see in the research in Part Two, an emotional connection with a brand can amplify the value of virtually any customer relationship.

Our goal as marketers is to achieve the highest possible connection with customers—the peak of the pyramid. To accomplish this connection, traditional marketing focuses on two areas—*how people feel* about a brand (the emotional connection) and *what people do* (transactions). (See Figure 2.2.)

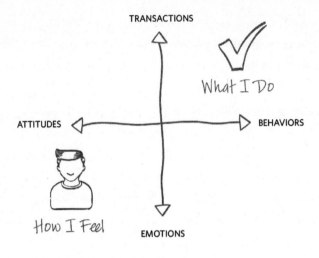

The Axis of Emotions and Actions

Figure 2.2 How consumers feel is reflected by their emotions, while what they do is recorded by their various actions and transactions. Understanding both areas is critical.

As we move through the book, we will be driving more deeply into the terms *experience* and *engagement*, exploring the individual data elements that measure them and looking at how they interoperate. But first, it's important to note that they come from two different perspectives, which have often been driven separately.

Experience: *How People Feel*—Emotional and Experiential Connections

How people feel about a brand—their emotional connection to a brand or product—can drive brand loyalty literally over generations. The almost incantatory power of brands—from Coca-Cola to Buick to Apple—stems largely from emotional connections created by effective advertising, strategic marketing, and customer experience. During the past 50 years, television images helped establish and amplify these emotional connections. Now constant consumer inundation with rich media online exponentially multiplies that emotional connection, since content can be shared easily, can go viral, and can reach a global audience in seconds—all at a much lower cost. On the Internet, emotions are easily shared, for better or for worse.

Traditional emotive communications could be loosely targeted through TV and print and customized based on geography and media. We all remember our favorite commercial or an ad that really made us feel like we wanted to be part of a brand. However, they were usually limited to mass media, bringing one message to a large number of customers. The overall emotional *experience* of a brand remains critically important. However, in this new world we have many more tools to choose from. We can still create beautiful, compelling content that connects with people. But now we can personalize it for an individual, have it endorsed by a friend, link it to a cause, or make it part of an exciting game or entertainment experience.

For example, Dove, a Unilever brand, discovered that only 2 percent of women consider themselves beautiful. So Dove created highly emotional experiences targeted at the other 98 percent to feel connected to the brand. Dove's *selfie campaign*, where women and their daughters posted and commented on photos, really worked for the Dove brand, with tens of thousands of women participating. That's an incredible emotional connection, one that creates powerful customer experiences.

Engagement: *What People Do*—Transactions as Connections

The other side of traditional marketing, a parallel practice, focuses on knowing *what people do*—their actions and transactions, in the physical world and online. Until recently, this area was about *what* and *when* people buy. This practice, which originated in transactional systems, market research, and direct marketing, allowed companies to understand specific customers and make a direct offer to them, encouraging them to buy a product or products. And it let brands understand directly if and when those customers buy.

These communications were inherently less about creating an emotional connection, and more focused on compelling consumers to exhibit the desired behavior—buying, calling, or responding. Now we have other transactions and responses—clicks, likes, referrals, shares, opt-ins, and more—that apply as well. These *upstream indicators* can create a much richer view of how customers interact with a brand.

For example, we recently worked with a retailer to identify the social media–using customers in its customer relationship management (CRM) database, and to explore their level of engagement. Our research and analysis showed that these customers were a gold mine. Any social engagement from a customer resulted in a 1.7 times increase in sales. And a customer who commented on the retailer's posts generated more than twice the sales of a non–socially engaged customer.

Customer Connections in the Current Era

These two types of connections, emotional and transactional, defined the old world of customer connections. But with the advent of new capabilities, brands now have the power to bring together the formerly separate worlds of experience responses (*how people feel*) and engagement (*what they do*). And we can do this in real time for each and every customer.

Technology is key to enabling this connection to happen. But beyond technology, connecting with customers means a new way of thinking, listening, organizing, and delivering a brand promise. In short, technology alone doesn't bring experience and engagement together. It requires a new approach to planning, executing, and measuring marketing.

As we'll see in Part Two of this book, our research shows that brands achieve real impact and measurable results when they bring together the combined, exponentially increased power of *what people do* and *how they feel*. It is this combination that ignites a customer connection—like flint and steel. It's all fueled by technology, from ubiquitous mobile communication to Big Data to social media, but the accelerants are your great ideas and a steady stream of powerful, compelling content.

Brands can deliver content via multiple channels, connecting with consumers how, where, and when they want. Content is data-driven and dynamic (if you want it to be), enabling a wildly different degree of agility never possible under the old limitations. Addressable media in search, display, e-mail, and even television expand the pool and accuracy of potential customer connections. Social media serves as a communication channel, of course, but also gives brands a sounding board to test and measure emotional connections.

Thanks to exponentially increasing consumer data and new ways of managing and accessing it, brands can record, store, access, and analyze consumer data in remarkably innovative ways. We can store vast amounts of information that can be accessed instantly. We can use machine learning to predict connections we could never think of with traditional marketing. And these capabilities are really just the beginning—there's much more ahead as marketers find new ways to tap Big Data to drive more effective marketing.

A Confluence of Capabilities Opens New Doors

Marketers have seen an incredible change during the past two years or so. Insights once available to only the deepest-pocketed brands are now widely available to and generally affordable for all brands.

Capabilities that once required major (and often proprietary) infrastructure investments—from databases to analytic software—are now available as a service on a pay-as-you-go model. And new players, from Facebook and LinkedIn to Pinterest and Snapchat, are now part of the team. They provide a platform to touch and connect with customers for a very low cost, leveling the playing field from the largest companies to the small businesses. The result? Game-changing capabilities.

For example, a major airline wanted to understand how members of its loyalty program interacted with the airline on social media. In the past, getting this level of detail might be difficult, if not impossible. But our digital analytics team matched loyalty members' e-mail addresses to their social URLs, and then analyzed the activity and sentiment of members' social postings.

The findings? Top-tier loyalty members were 111 percent more likely to be socially engaged and 540 percent more likely to be discussion shapers. And to show how social engagement affected purchasing engagement, the median 12-month spend for social engagers was 6.7 percent greater than for nonengagers. Data like this, and plenty more of it, helps brands know their customers better.

As Always, Knowledge Is Power

Today, brands know more about customers—their emotions and transactions—than ever before. But translating that knowledge into actionable insights and real and lasting customer connections remains the pressing challenge facing marketers. After all, we are still in the early days of developing strategies that address how best to harness the positive possibilities and avoid the negative ones. But the level of proficiency and fluency in next-generation marketing continues to grow as more and more marketers leave the traditional behind and embrace new opportunities.

One of the key opportunities as we see it is to create what we call *atomic moments of truth*. They may sound unusual, but they're incredibly important to successful marketing in the new era. We'll take a closer look at them in the next chapter.

Customer Connections

- There are many levels of customer connection —brands want closer/deeper connections.

- EXPERIENCE reflects the emotional connection—how customers feel.

- ENGAGEMENT reflects actions (buy, like, other)—what consumers do.

- Bringing together these two elements creates positive business outcomes.

- The combination isn't incremental; it's exponential—ROE^2.

Chapter 3
Atomic Moments of Truth

They're Small and Plentiful, and Have the Power to Make or Break Your Brand

N ow that we have examined the elements of a strong customer connection, we will look to how you activate those connections in the market. The notion of a linear customer journey and monolithic buying decision, one that marketers are constantly nudging consumers toward, is no longer an accurate portrayal of reality. The new marketing landscape requires new ways of thinking about consumers. The fact is that consumers are communicating all the time—with brands and with each other. They're looking for information, generating feedback, commenting on brands, and buying products. Right now. And I like to call each of these tiny decisions an *atomic moment of truth*. Here we take a look at atomic moments of truth, where they can happen, and some of the challenges that marketers face in this new, atomized world.

The Power to Create or Destroy Value

Harnessing the power of these moments is the goal for marketers now and in the coming decade. Every atomic moment of truth is an

Atomic Moments of Truth

Figure 3.1   Marketers need to recognize which specific atomic moments of truth inspire their customers, and take advantage of all opportunities.

opportunity for a brand to understand and impact engagement and experience, and to create value for a customer (and for the brand)—or to destroy it. In this context, winning requires handling each consumer interaction—and there are many of them—in such a way that it creates value. As we'll see, it's a challenge, given the diversity and sheer volume of these moments.

Know an Atomic Moment of Truth When You See One

To harness the brand-building potential of an atomic moment of truth, you have to first recognize it *when* and *where* it is happening.

To start, accept that all consumer interactions, online and offline, represent potential atomic moments of truth. These moments come in different forms—identifiable and anonymous, inbound and outbound, static and interactive, batch and real-time. But they all represent an opportunity to advance and enhance the incremental continuum of communication and connection that has replaced the monolithic buying decision. In short, atomic moments of truth matter because they lead to better things—great brand loyalty, product purchases, recommendations, and more.

Here are three scenarios to consider:

1. **A call center rep** is on the phone with a valuable customer who has been researching a new category purchase but is frustrated with the online experience. What should the rep do to turn this atomic moment of truth into a customer connection?

2. **A major retailer** sends an e-mail to a customer at 6 a.m. The customer opens the e-mail on her smartphone, clicks through to the mobile site, and engages with the site but doesn't buy anything. What should the next communication be to get the best possible outcome from an atomic moment of truth?

3. **A fan** (with lots of followers) of a major sports league posts a tweet talking about the health and safety risks of the sport for children.

Answers:

1. The rep should ignore any goals in terms of calls taken per hour to work with the client to resolve his online experience or take the order over the phone. Then the rep should send a follow-up e-mail making sure the customer has everything he needs.

2. The retailer should retarget that customer when she is likely to be opening her e-mail on her desktop.

3. Curate the Twitter feed to look for references (positive or negative) and tweets from the commissioner's office about what is being done from a health and safety perspective.

In each of these cases it would easy (and common) for a brand to be passive and unresponsive. But when each of these interactions is viewed as an atomic moment of truth with an opportunity to impact Experience × Engagement and business value, you can recognize that the consumers have provided you with valuable information about what they are doing or how they feel—the kind of insights that can be leveraged to create brand and business equity.

A Closer Look at Atomic Moments of Truth

Why do we call them *atomic*? Atomic is a word that plays both ways. It describes the scale of matter down to the smallest level, hinting at the plentitude and ubiquity of these moments. And on the more volatile side, it hints at atomic energy, good or bad, by which energy is exponentially increased to generate power—or a nuclear explosion. Our referencing of this dichotomy, good power versus destructive power, is intentional, as you'll see.

Why do we call them *moments*? Well, a moment is a tiny increment of time, not a loaded juncture that everything depends upon. Life is made up of billions of moments and tiny decisions that guide our lives. So it is with the marketplace. Our choice of the word *moment* is simply our recognition that there are lots of chances to build or destroy value. All are equally important.

Why do we call them moments of *truth*? Because after all is said and done, no marketer can take action *for* a consumer. Consumers have to do it themselves. And all the input, encouragement, and enticement possible via marketing come down to a moment of truth when the consumer acts—buying a product, recommending it, committing to the brand, providing feedback, connecting with the brand. That's the truth of it.

The Moment Is Momentous

I met with an interesting company recently, FootClicks, which takes the *moment of truth* concept all the way to the store aisle. Its proprietary technology lets stores send personalized messages and content to customers in the stores (via their smartphones)—right in the aisle at the moment of truth when customers are making their purchase decisions. This capability, long a dream of retailers (the crude version—the in-store loudspeaker), is now a very sophisticated reality. "Consumers often reserve final decision making until they are in front of a product," says Dan Stanek, president and chief client officer. "You have to be able to connect with the customer at that exact moment. It's just not effective enough anymore to send an offer to their homes and expect them to go to the stores. You have to engage with them and influence them right in the store at the moment of truth by delivering relevant information, the right offer, and facts that help them differentiate a line of products."

The same approach holds true online as it does in stores. The atomic moment of truth is a critical point of interaction.

The Moment Starts with Customer Awareness

The reality is that, in some cases, you will have a deep knowledge about customers—what they need, want, and prefer. And you'll have a good idea about the best way to optimize an interaction. In other cases, a customer profile will be very opaque. You may know little more about the customer than a cookie or an e-mail address. However, in today's world, you can infer and leverage data in these cases, taking the knowledge deeper and creating more meaningful connections than those apparent in the data explicitly stated or collected from consumers.

For example, an Internet Protocol (IP) address can geolocate a customer, a cookie (or the mobile equivalent) can give you information about what the person is doing online, and matching that cookie with available first- and third-party data can add more detail and context. Authentication with an e-mail address ensures that there's a real opportunity. So in less than 100 milliseconds, you might be able to find out that your prospect is 34, lives in Kansas City, has two kids, is enrolled in a customer loyalty program, and buys three HP 53A toner cartridges once a month. With this information, the company could infer (or algorithmically predict) that this is a tech-savvy consumer. They could target a display ad for a next-generation printer, post an ad for computers for the prospect's children on the Facebook exchange, and follow up both ads with an e-mail message that explains the value in loyalty points if the customer responded to both offers.

If you could go back a decade in time and show these kinds of capabilities to old-school marketers, their heads might very well explode.

Understand the Value in Play

As we saw in the prior chapter, understanding the customer is important, but not enough. Every atomic moment of truth represents an opportunity to create or destroy value. (See Figure 3.2.) It's important to understand the value in play, and what's at stake. *Value* is a slippery word that implies financial value, but can mean much more. Value has multiple dimensions, including:

- The current financial value of customers—what they can buy now
- The potential value of customers—what they are spending with competitors
- The emotional equity that a customer has with your brand
- The network/influencer effect of a customer (via social networks)
- The value (positive or negative) of fulfilling or breaking a brand promise

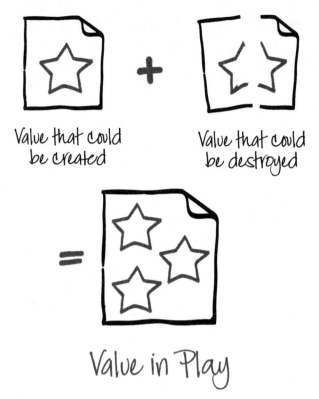

Value that could be created

Value that could be destroyed

Value in Play

Figure 3.2 Value is multidimensional. Knowing the value that you can gain (or lose) helps you allocate your marketing spend accordingly.

Invest the Appropriate Time and Money

No two moments offer the same value—knowing a moment's potential is critical to knowing how much time and/or spend to devote to it. These investments come in many forms:

- Time (e.g., time spent on a customer phone call or meeting)
- Incentives
- Rewards
- Discounts
- Content

- Information and expertise (general or proprietary)
- Community—creating connections for customers
- Number of touches or impressions

In addition, factor in the opportunity cost of irrelevance (i.e., the long-term cost of irrelevant messaging to drive short-term gains). For example, when a retailer e-mails about a one-day sale for 30 days in a row, it can have a negative impact.

What's an Opportunity Worth?

Ask yourself how much you would invest in:

- A high-value customer who placed a phone call with your brand that offered little incremental sales potential but a strong potential to influence
- A low-value customer who hasn't purchased anything yet but seems to be a strong supporter of your brand
- An industry commentator who is looking to get attention from your brand in exchange for promoting it to his 50,000 Twitter followers

These scenarios and more point out the need to know, often on the fly, how much time, energy, and/or money to invest in an opportunity—because they are not created equal anymore.

Building Blocks for Managing Atomic Moments of Truth

Creating atomic moments of truth needs to be a systematic, repeatable process. After all, you want moments, not a moment. There are many key enablers necessary to manage these moments:

- **Identification.** The capability to understand the consumer's identity can come from a consumer authenticating in a channel, by using a cookie match, or by relying on other techniques to understand and identify consumers in an unauthenticated state.

- **Intelligence.** The capability to understand customers as they are communicating to or about your brand includes information that is part of the iterations (e.g., what page of the website they are on), third-party data (e.g., demographics or buying propensities), and first-party data that customers have provided via purchasing or preferences.

- **Data management.** A way to manage customer data centrally via data services requires access to deep historical stores of data but also will require data that can be used for decisions in real time.

- **Real-time decision making.** There are real-time data tools that can decide what the right message is with a subsecond response.

- **Content management.** There must be a way to create and manage content so that it can be dynamically assembled and delivered in a channel-agnostic manner.

- **A clear record of interactions.** A key element of an atomic moment of truth is that each moment also generates new data. So there must be a way to collect information that consumers are generating with every interaction and then feed it into the next interaction. (See Figure 3.3.)

Clearly, having all of these elements in place for all customers and all channels can be an enormous task. Organizations need to prioritize their key channels and products to align capabilities (and investments) accordingly. And while many brands see the capabilities as a technology challenge, the unavailability or high expense of technology is no longer an excuse for sticking with status-quo marketing. But as we explore next, critical pain points remain for marketing organizations.

Record of Interactions

Figure 3.3   Every interaction with a consumer generates data that must be stored, analyzed, and put to work to inform and improve the next interaction.

The Top Challenges Today's Marketers Face

Significant advancements in many of the capabilities and technologies are fueling a major and ongoing digital disruption in marketing. However, they also raise four critical business issues: broken processes, islands of information, inaccurate measurement, and using yesterday's creative approach.

1. Broken Processes

Campaigns were typically planned and executed in a linear fashion with traditional work flow and project

(continued)

management approaches. These solutions worked when brands had a small number of campaigns active at any given time. With the possibility of millions of campaigns running simultaneously, these approaches break down. And increasing the number of vendors involved in the marketing process—from ideation to execution—creates tremendous complexity.

2. Islands of Information

The proliferation of channels creates a new archipelago of islands of information. Most brands use different technologies to manage each channel—each with its own data store. These islands create clear issues when marketers want to execute and analyze an effective multichannel campaign.

3. Inaccurate Measurement

Traditionally, measurement is based on *last click* or *last touch* approaches that attribute credit for a sale. As the pace and complexity of marketing ramp up, these approaches fall short. In the new world, companies have to focus on *causality*—which interaction or combination of interactions caused a sale or change in consumer behavior. And they have to address *incrementality*—was this change in behavior actually incremental or would it have happened anyway?

4. Yesterday's Creative Approach

The creative team must step up its game and recognize the new realities of marketing. Content must be customized versus a one-size-fits-all approach. In fact, 78 percent of chief marketing officers (CMOs) see custom content as the future of marketing, according to WebDAM Marketing Trends for 2014. The creative team must take advantage of low-cost, personalized video and other advances. And it

(continued)

must make an emotional connection—the key to creating atomic moments of truth.

None of these challenges is insurmountable, of course. But none should be taken lightly, either.

Inspiring Hotel Happiness

To conclude this chapter, I'd like to pass along a brief story about how Epsilon recently helped a global hotel chain harness atomic moments of truth to uncover more value from its loyalty program members. This legendary brand wanted to improve its customer experience and capture increased share of wallet across its global, multibrand organization, which spans 2,800 properties, nine brands, and more than 350 partners.

We worked closely with the hotel chain to create a marketing solution that gives the company the ability to notify consumers online, via e-mail, on mobile devices, and when they are on a property—all opportunities to create atomic moments of truth. It integrates data from the interaction point with first- and third-party customer data, as well as with property management information (e.g., the capacity of a specific hotel), and then delivers specific, timely content to that customer.

Content includes discounts, offers to use additional services, and general information that can improve the quality of a stay. Versions of the content are created based on past history, the loyalty of a customer, the customer's disposition during the interaction, and analysis of the needs and wants of similar clients.

The results? Share of member wallet has grown from 40 percent to 64 percent. The program has scaled from 425 to 2,800 hotels and from 16 to 350 partners. It includes 10 million active members and 12,000 active program bonuses. And it performs 950 million computations daily—in real time, across more than 350 airline, retail, financial, and award partners. And it's still going strong.

What does this story show us? Atomic moments of truth can happen via multiple channels—and they can deliver significant bottom-line results.

Atomic Moments of Truth

- Atomic moments of truth inspire consumers to take action.

- The right offer, right time, personalization—it inspires action.

- Marketers can understand and impact Experience × Engagement—and create or destroy value.

- Marketers should align their investment in a customer to the "value in play."

- Inspiring atomic moments of truth requires deep customer knowledge.

- Atomic moments of truth are happening all the time.

Chapter 4
The Amplification Effect

Multiply the Power of Experience ✕ Engagement

W e've explored how customers feel about a brand (experience) and how they interact with a brand (engagement) in real time via various channels. These two elements are more than two different ways that brands connect with customers. They are the ways that *customer connections* happen. In Part Two, we will see empirical evidence that improving experience and engagement creates a multiplicative effect on the financial performance of customers and the communications that touch them. Here we explore how the powerful combination of Experience ✕ Engagement represents a fundamentally new model for marketing—and for planning and allocating your marketing budget.

Defining Experience ✕ Engagement

Let's start by taking a closer look at the terms used to define customer connection—*experience* and *engagement*. The words are used loosely in a variety of marketing contexts and are often misused and confused. It's important to establish a canonical definition, since it informs the

research in the remainder of this book. Here are the definitions that we
have established for *Igniting Customer Connections*:

- *Experience* **means the emotional connection with a brand.** *How
  does it make you feel? Will your life be easier or your self-esteem higher?
  Will you have more friends?* Experience is at the heart of the basic
  drive that consumers feel to try a brand, to purchase a brand, and
  to become loyal to that brand.

- *Engagement* **means acting.** Actions that the consumer can take
  include buying, posting, tweeting, liking, following, referring, and
  more. But all require consumers to do something tangible that
  engages them with a brand.

Where Do You Find Experience and Engagement?

How do you take the concepts of engagement and experience and integrate them into your day-to-day marketing? It's the age-old challenge of
turning theory into practice. One way to make these inherently abstract
concepts more real is to take a closer look at the elements comprising
experience and engagement—and the specific channels and areas where
experience and engagement happen.

Imagine trying to make sense of an inherently vague concept like
happiness, particularly if you were arriving on our planet from a much less
emotional solar system. You might have a general sense of what happiness was. But a real understanding wouldn't happen until you dug more
deeply and examined what happiness was made up of (*elements*, from a
general sense of well-being to complete bliss) and the places where happiness might occur (*channels*, from holiday gatherings to golf courses).

Applying the Amplification Effect

Is the combination of experience and engagement a $1 + 1 = 2$ proposition? I don't think so. My experience tells me that a more rational and

accurate hypothesis would be that combining experience with engagement is a $1 \times 1 = 5$ proposition. Or, more accurately, it reflects an exponential multiplying of the two elements—in short, it's a much more transformational than incremental concept. For example, in Part Two of this book you will see that highly engaged consumers who also feel an emotional connection with the brand are 2,233 percent more likely to have bought in the prior three months. This extreme example shows the power of Return on Experience $\times$ Engagement (ROE^2).

We'll be presenting more proprietary research and real-world customer stories that show and measure the impact of Experience $\times$ Engagement. But first, we need to explore a concept that puts Experience $\times$ Engagement into action—the *actionable brand idea* (ABI).

What Is an Actionable Brand Idea?

Think of *actionable brand ideas* as the connective tissue between experience and engagement. (See Figure 4.1.) Developing actionable brand ideas is key to connecting the two realms—experience (*what you feel*) with engagement (*what you do*). A breakthrough marketing strategy is manifested in an actionable brand or business idea that is activated throughout the customer journey, igniting engaging customer experiences that achieve the desired results. These ideas are the ultimate goal of marketers, since they represent both creativity (ideas) and business results, while staying completely focused on the brand.

A Closer Look at an Actionable Business Idea

The best way to describe an actionable business idea is to take a look at one—where it came from, how it evolved, and its impact. A few years ago, FedEx was considering launching a new loyalty program. Its objective? FedEx wanted to consolidate market share from other shipping providers. FedEx had endless amounts of data about what

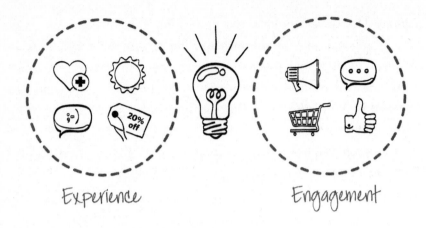

Experience   Engagement

Actionable Brand Ideas

Figure 4.1 Actionable brand ideas connect experience and engagement and lead the way to building brand and business equity.

small businesses were doing with their services and also had a significant amount of information about the needs of small businesses by industry. For example, auto parts dealers need low-cost freight services whereas lawyers and accountants need fast overnight and before 10 a.m. services.

FedEx was great at doing traditional marketing that delivered messages around the core value of its services, and price incentives to help consolidate market share. However, that wasn't enough to change customer behavior. The company needed to connect emotionally with potential customers and give them a reason to consider (or reconsider) a switch to FedEx.

With its core industry focus, FedEx set out to try to find a way to connect with these customers—to find out what would get a small business owner excited, and what would create perceived value greater than the actual value. What the company found was not really surprising.

Auto parts dealers love NASCAR, lawyers and accountants like golf, and so on. The brilliance of the FedEx strategy was that when it looked for the right way to foster a strong connection via *experience*, it found that its event sponsorships with PGA, the NFL, and NASCAR provided a wealth of award opportunities that would create that emotional connection between FedEx and its customers.

FedEx used these relationships to provide the opportunity for an auto parts dealer to earn the chance to get its logo on a car during a NASCAR race—and other incentives that connected customers to the brand on a very emotional level. The result? The program generated millions of dollars in incremental sales for FedEx.

The Impact of Timing on Experience × Engagement

As every actor, musician, or comedian knows, timing is everything. So it is for marketing. The dynamic of time is critical, and it affects and amplifies the cumulative impact in several critical ways:

- **Making the connection.** As we discussed in the context of atomic moments of truth, the ability to construct an effective, dynamic message in real time is critical. This message can help bring both elements—experience and engagement—together for each customer. These elements are deeply interrelated and, when they come together in the right way, an atomic moment of truth is created that's more powerful than one simple touch point.

- **Using cadence and frequency.** As marketers, we use deep analysis to optimize timing for many of the interactions along a nonlinear purchase path. We decide when a campaign runs and how many times we touch a customer. We decide how frequently we post on social media. So it's important to identify the right cadence and frequency that resonate with your target audience. Too much contact in a short period can make recipients feel besieged by marketing, triggering possible opt outs. Too much time between contacts can cause you to risk losing momentum. Each group you market to will have its own preferred pacing. It's critical to identify and respect these preferences.

- **Taking the long view.** It's important to point out that driving experience and engagement doesn't happen via a single interaction or exposure. It's an ongoing process—the cumulative effect of many touches with a consumer. As marketers, we need to recognize the flow of time and consider the longer-term goals when adaptively planning the flow of connections with consumers.

Measurement: Beyond Return on Investment

By establishing experience and engagement as key indicators of customer connection, we start to rethink return on investment (ROI) as the core and/or only way of measuring success. I've spent a fair amount of time considering ROI, which I believe to be an inadequate and incomplete way to measure marketing success in our era—when campaigns, channels, customer touch points, and other key elements of marketing have grown exponentially in complexity and velocity.

ROI is DOA. That would be the most attention-getting way to think about ROI. But my thinking about ROI is a bit more realistic—ROI is an ingrained staple in business and marketing, and it's not going away. That said, it's limited in that it looks at cost and performance over a defined period of time, one that is often linked to a campaign. The time-based nature of ROI means it has several inherent shortcomings:

- **No communication costs.** It ignores the cumulative effect (cost and return) of communications over time.

- **No experience.** It does not measure the critical impact—or cause and effect—of experience and how that may connect a consumer and brand over time.

- **Old approach.** It is linked to the increasingly antiquated concept of a marketing campaign calendar or cycle.

- **Short-term thinking.** It can lead to short-term decisions that are financially prudent at the time, but do not allocate marketing funds to drive long-term results.

- **No measuring of lost opportunities.** It ignores the (lost) opportunity cost of annoying a consumer forever.

ROI: A Venerable Concept

A young man named Donaldson Brown joined DuPont in 1909 to sell more explosives. In 1912, he submitted a legendary efficiency report to his corporate masters that used a new

(continued)

"return on investment" formula. This report led to a type of accounting and a common and consistent way of interpreting and comparing investments based on their performance—in short, an apples-to-apples comparison. ROI reduced any investment down to a common denominator that enabled management to envision results across a wide range of investments, since DuPont was an investor in diverse technologies, from gunpowder to automobiles.

ROI's origins create its limitations. It's reductive. It treats all investments equally. And it's based on well-defined periods of slow-moving time (in 1912), making it much more relevant to the turn of the previous century than today.

The Shortcomings of ROI

Many years ago I worked with a credit card company that was doing an extensive amount of direct mail to maximize the value of its customers. We did an inventory of the direct mail that consumers would get over a year, and it covered a large kitchen table. The company had a rigorous, ROI-based approach to how it planned and allocated marketing funds. Furthermore, it planned based on product groups. For example, the product manager for credit card insurance had a highly tuned, analytically based process to get customers to buy the credit card insurance, and proved that the company could mail four waves of the credit card insurance mailing and by the fourth and final wave enough customers would have responded to generate positive ROI.

The challenge came when we stepped back and asked the client about its actionable brand/business idea, which was: *Don't compartmentalize*. For example, don't use one card for business and another card for personal expenses. And when we looked at all the communications with a positive ROI, none of them were promoting that actionable business idea. They were all selling a single product to drive short-term ROI—but ignoring the larger opportunity.

What's the moral of this story? Short-term gains can come at the expense of longer-term, more valuable customer connections.

The Marketing Calendar Is History

Many of us who have spent years as marketing practitioners have lived and died by the *campaign calendar*, which used to define the strategy, content, and tempo of marketing campaigns. It came from a time when we ran a small fixed number of campaigns a year, requiring weeks (or in some cases, months) to plan, produce, and measure. These campaigns were usually single-channel campaigns (e.g., the media calendar was largely separate from the direct marketing calendar), and they were generally only responsive to prior results over long periods of time.

Fast forward to today, and it's a whole new world. I work with clients and even individual marketing managers that may have thousands (or millions) of campaigns running at all times. Responding to real-time or near real-time analytics, these clients are continually refining audience definitions, content, and channels. They are not predicting these marketing campaigns weeks or months in advance, but responding to what consumers are doing every day.

Figure 4.2   Today's marketers have to manage multiple campaigns, reach out via multiple channels, and deal with a remarkably fast pace of change.

Turning Knowledge into Strategies

We've explored the ideas of experience and engagement, as well as atomic moments of truth and actionable business ideas. All these concepts may leave you wondering: *How can I put this information to work within my organization?* In the next chapter, we turn to clear strategies you can leverage to transform your marketing, connect with customers, and optimize your marketing dollars by keeping your spending focused on the channels and segments that get results.

The Amplification Effect

- Experience × Engagement delivers an amplified result.

- The combination of these two consumer behaviors is powerful.

- Time is a critical element of optimizing experience and engagement.

- Actionable, informed business ideas inspire action.

- ROI is an inherently limited way to measure results.

- ROE^2 addresses the challenges of measuring results in a digital world.

Chapter 5
A Closer Look at ROE^2

Get a Clear Summary of ROE^2—and a *For-Mere-Mortals* Look at the Math Behind It

H ere we take a closer look at Return on Experience × Engagement (ROE^2) and its elements, and provide a more detailed view of how it works. And we explore the math behind our approach to inspiring and measuring ROE^2.

As we discussed in the previous chapters of Part One, ROE^2 starts with an actionable brand idea (ABI). An organization will develop its actionable brand ideas by looking at the macro context of the *Five Cs*—context, category, competition, company, and customer. ABIs are informed by this information and in particular by knowledge of customers and their needs, and are focused on the customer behaviors the organization seeks and the attributes it can influence.

Here are some of my favorite examples of ABIs:

- **TXU**—*Use less of what I sell.* Instead of focusing on price, this energy company focused the consumers on paying less based on managing usage.

- **Dove**—*Beauty as a source of confidence, not anxiety.* Instead of using models, Dove created a social campaign that encouraged consumers to upload photos of themselves—selfies with a purpose.

- **Mead**—*Quality and durability that is legendary.* This ABI drove the Cinco the Dog campaign (the dog that can't eat the homework)—a great piece of engaging content.

A well-conceived ABI will facilitate the creation of customer experiences and engagement that strengthen connection to the brand—and drive improved business outcomes in the form of greater brand and business equity (ROE^2). But in an era of snackable infographics, what does ROE^2 really look like? (See Figure 5.1.)

The Promise of ROE^2

When a company consistently delivers positive engagement and experiences and better connects with customers, it will realize sustainable

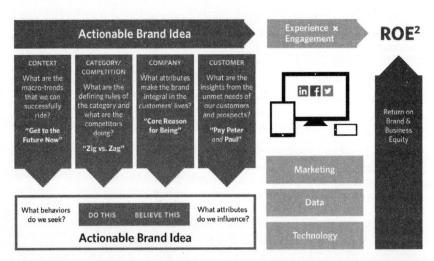

Figure 5.1 ROE^2 starts with an actionable brand idea that triggers positive consumer experience and engagement, leading to a higher return on brand and business equity.

business growth. Before we get into Part Two of the book—where we share powerful case studies and data-driven research on how ROE² works—we need to clarify and confirm the components of ROE².

ROE² Defined

Return on Experience × Engagement = Improved Brand and Business Equity

But how do you separate these often conflated or confused terms?

- **Experience** is *how consumers feel*—how the brand comes to life for the customer and the emotions it evokes.

- **Engagement** is *what they do*—how the customer interacts with the brand through touch points, and receptivity, reaction to, and collaboration with those touch points.

And how do we measure and/or observe experience and engagement? There are various dimensions to both concepts, so let's look at some examples. (See Figure 5.2.)

It's important to recognize that measures of experience and engagement vary by industry as well as by company. In short, your definition of experience and engagement needs to be considered in the context of your business. The metrics should be specific to how your company runs its business and what you are trying to achieve with your customers—and how you are going about it. That said, the list in Figure 5.2 has broad applicability and serves a useful starting point for most companies as they set out to gauge their own customers' experiences and engagement.

A Closer Look at Returns—the Final Result

If ROE² is Return on Experience × Engagement, we also need a way to measure *return*—the ultimate results that ROE² delivers. The return is defined in terms of desired business outcomes—specifically, measures

Take a Closer Look at Emotion and Engagement

Experience/Emotion	Engagement
Customer service staff is friendly	Responded to a survey
Customer service staff is responsive	Opted in to receive e-mails
Customer service is knowledgeable	Opened/clicked on an e-mail
Products/services are of high quality	Unsubscribed from e-mail
Provides good value for the money	Called the customer service center
Provides a range of products/services that meet my needs	Called an 800 # in response to e-mail or direct mail
Problems are resolved quickly	Followed the brand on Twitter
I am never disappointed by this brand	Liked the brand on Facebook
Is a leader/highly respected in its category	Referred others to the brand
Has a good public image	Searched online for the brand
Has values consistent with mine	Downloaded a brand app
Treats me like an individual	Read an online review of the brand
Is innovative	Posted an online review
Is trustworthy	Visited the company website
Is socially responsible	Used a web-based preference center
Is accessible	Entered a sweepstakes
Is easy to do business with/convenient	
Has a great rewards program	
Had good or memorable advertising	

Figure 5.2　Here are some general examples of experience and engagement. While most engagement measures are positive, some are negative, and it's equally important to track these.

of brand and business equity. Again, these will vary by company, based on the objectives of your organization.

Shown in Figure 5.3 is a set of established brand and business equity measures that provides a solid and varied candidate list for consideration by your company.

About Brand and Business Equity

Brand Equity	Business Equity
Customer satisfaction	Share of wallet
Purchase and repurchase intent	Share-of-wallet intent
Brand commitment/affinity	Customer spending
Likelihood to recommend (net promoter)	Customer retention
Brand advocacy	Customer profitability
	Customer lifetime value

Figure 5.3 Here are some general examples of brand and business equity measures. Note that advocacy can take many forms—examples include liking the brand on Facebook, posting a positive online review of the brand, blog posts, forwarding a brand's e-mails, referring others to the brand, and so on.

As you can see, brand equity and business equity are measured at the consumer level. But Return on Experience × Engagement will manifest itself in another, more visible and important way—as your brand wins the battle for the consumer, company profitability and shareholder value ultimately rise as well. This is the final barometer of the success of your company's strategy for increasing ROE².

The Math Behind ROE²

Throughout Part One of this book, we have established the elements of ROE² and discussed how they work and fit together in general terms. The basic premise is that positive engagement and experience lead to better business outcomes—in the form of improvements in brand and business equity. Here we take a closer look at the math behind ROE²—for more analytical and mathematical readers.

(continued)

How do we establish this linkage between experience and engagement and brand and business equity? The answers lies in a tried-and-true statistical tool called *multiple regression analysis*. Regression analysis is a technique used to determine how a set of variables or factors explain or predict an outcome variable of interest. It essentially creates an algorithm that quantifies the relationship between the explanatory variables and the outcome variable.

In mathematical terms, it looks like this:

$$ROE^2 = f(EX_i + EN_i + O_i)$$

where:

ROE^2 = measures of brand and business equity (the outcome variable)

EX_i = measures of customer experience

EN_i = measures of customer engagement

O_i = other variables that influence ROE^2

Regression analysis not only tells us what variables are predictive of ROE^2 but also tells us the *relative* importance of each. This insight becomes useful information for marketing practitioners as you try to determine how to invest in various activities that boost customer experience and engagement. By doing so, you can plan more intelligently and achieve better returns on related investments. For example, the chart in Figure 5.4 shows the relative impact of the experiential variables of ROE^2 in the hospitality industry, which we explore in much more detail in Chapter 10.

Figure 5.4 In this example, brand and business equity are defined as brand commitment and share-of-wallet intent.

A Look Ahead at How ROE² Triggers Better Business Outcomes

The research we are about to explore in Part Two of this book will illustrate how various measures of experience and engagement explain or predict brand and business equity and quantify their relative importance. As shown in Figure 5.4, these particular regression models identified a total of eight contributing factors. The top three drivers— alignment, recognition, and stature—collectively explained 58 percent of the variation in brand and business equity.

While marketing is often fueled by qualitative theories and techniques, ROE² is a quantifiable, measurable attribute that provides a clear reflection of the importance of Experience × Engagement—and provides powerful inspiration to marketers to focus on these key areas.

Chapter 6
Strategies for Transformation

Clear, Achievable Next Steps Help You Start Igniting Customer Connections *Now*

W e've shown that marketing is in a period of unprecedented change. We've described how connecting with customers requires taking a new approach to all aspects of marketing, from building customer value to measuring results by understanding engagement and experience. The reality? Implementing these approaches can be incredibly simple or very complex, depending on how you go about it. So how can you turn what you've learned into actionable, day-to-day strategies and results? Here we conclude Part One with four key strategies that you can use to start igniting new connections with your customers— no matter how small or large your organization and no matter what industry you're in.

1. Rethink measurement.

2. Organize around the customer, not products or channels.

3. Establish a consistent marketing process.

4. Use technology to enable, not distract.

Rethink Measurement

I've described how the old approaches to measurement are no longer sufficient, and how the approach we call Return on Experience × Engagement (ROE^2) is a more useful way of evaluating marketing efforts. So rethinking measurement is a good place to start when describing go-forward strategies you can start implementing quickly. Focusing on outcomes means beginning with the end in mind, always a challenge for marketers, who can get consumed and distracted by creation and implementation.

To revisit the past briefly, measurement used to be at the end of what marketers generally treated as a linear progression of:

- Analysis and insights
- Planning and creative work
- Testing
- Execution and measurement

This linear process is based on the old marketing environment, when there were fewer campaigns and each took a longer time to execute. And it involved measurement using the old standby, return on investment (ROI). But it's important to rethink this approach.

Why? Because measurement isn't at the end of the line anymore. Measurement, analysis, and segmentation are three very interdependent concepts that are bound together throughout any marketing effort—from start to finish and back again. It's the basis of analysis that may trigger more insights and inspire new strategies. How can you rethink measurement? We advocate taking the following steps with your marketing:

- **Measure results**, not just for a campaign, but for every key communication (atomic moment of truth), piece of content, channel, and instance of delivery. In short, expand the scope of what you're measuring.

- **Eliminate** nonperforming content and interactions, and promote performers when evaluating your marketing.
- **Ask** why what happened did happen. Look for the root causes of why a communication or strategy is not performing.
- **Use the findings** to make changes to your strategies.

Start (and End) with the Customer

As part of your rethinking of measurement, map the *decision space,* formerly the much more linear *point of purchase.* Recent research we commissioned specifically for this book shows that there are many different paths and influences that lead a consumer to make a buying decision.

Now that it's no longer linear, the purchase decision may involve a more complicated path. There may be multiple paths. Or it may not resemble a path at all, and be more like entering a decision zone. But you need to be ready when the customer gets there. And you need to ensure that you're spending only on the most important nodes (channels and beyond) that have proven (via measurement) to move the journey ahead.

Good Customers Aren't Your Only Customers

When rethinking measurement, it's important to expand your view—and the focus of your measurement and analysis—beyond good customers. After all, customers with a lot of potential to become good customers are equally important to your future.

(continued)

- Look at behaviors that you want consumers to exhibit (open, click, buy, tweet, like, refer, publish).

- Model what your best customers do in terms of each of these behaviors.

- Apply those models across your customers (or prospects) and determine who could do more.

Organize around the Customer, Not Products or Channels

Igniting new customer connections requires taking a careful look at your organization and making changes that eliminate organizational or technological silos or roadblocks. For example, organize around your target segments—and how you fulfill their needs most effectively. This advice may sound obvious, but there are many ways to distract organizational attention. Many companies organize and group their customers by products (e.g., shoppers for home furnishings, sports, or apparel) or channels (people who shop in the store or online). Those groupings and lenses are often necessary but not sufficient. Until you look at a customer holistically, you will not be able optimize the relationship.

Getting your organization right is critical. And that means making changes that keep you relentlessly focused on meeting customer needs and reaching segments—and optimizing customer relations, not just product silos or channels.

As part of focusing on the customer, access to data needs to be streamlined and open, since centralized data is an enabler for all. Data ownership and protection are critical today—but the ability to leverage data quickly will be a competitive differentiator in the future. After all, transactions are information, whether it's the fact that someone purchased something, posted on Facebook, opened an e-mail, or complained to customer service. Key groups and people in your organization need to be able to access *all* of this information in a way so that it can be correlated quickly and easily. So tear down the product or channel walls that can blind an organization and keep it from seeing new opportunities to connect with customers.

People Make Customer Connections

Data is important in our increasingly digital world. But people make your brand what it is. Trust your staff—and your customers—to represent your brand. These people may be consumers, advocates, fans, or friends, or they may be detractors, gadflies, and critics. But they are the ones who know the most about your brand. So they need to be rock solid in their commitment to it. Your staff/employees are vital, of course. It may sound harsh, but *if your employees haven't bought in, buy them out.*

The Role of Values

Think about your own values and how they play out through the customer experience. As part of your ongoing focus on your customer, consider establishing a customer-focused values system. For example, Zappos did extraordinarily well with "Customer delight is always right." By driving this values system throughout your enterprise, you take an important step toward igniting customer connections. *How* and *why* you do it are even more important than exactly *what* you do. Apple is, of course, the gold standard for valuing the customer throughout the organization, from product development to the Genius Bar.

Starting to Ignite New Connections

With your organization aligned behind meeting customer needs and focused on your key segments, you're reading to start igniting customer connections. Driving deeper connections starts with uncovering the most important and high-impact branches of the proverbial customer decision tree. Evaluate your success by taking a clear, hard look at how well each marketing effort you implement drives high-value customers higher up the relationship pyramid we established in Chapter 2 (see Figure 6.1). And make it clear to all new (and veteran) marketers that their primary job is to manage trust and influence relationships—a task that goes beyond traditional campaigns and quarterly targets.

Figure 6.1   Your marketing initiatives should be focused on driving more high-value customers up the pyramid that represents the Hierarchy of Connections.

Establish a Consistent Marketing Process

The current marketing landscape is evolving quickly, creating the need for a consistent process that lets you keep pace and evolve along with it. A marketing process can seem to be about the steps you take to execute a communication, but it's really about how to allocate your dollars to the customers and prospects that have the greatest ability to drive value (brand and business equity). It's critical to have a common way that these decisions are made, as well as how different techniques, strategies, and content are tested. And, of course, you need a consistent way to measure—no matter who or what the customer, channel, or content may be. Using ROE^2 as an approach with your key drivers of business outcomes will be an important part of that link. When creating the process that will keep your marketing moving ahead and igniting new customer connections, keep these general directives in mind:

- **Adapt.** The new digital channels offer an unprecedented ability to test and learn, often virtually in real time. Take advantage of the chance to do some informed experimentation. It may be uncomfortable, but try testing all elements: segments, content, and channels. If you focus on getting in the market quickly, you may save yourself a lot of time and spark new ideas from your customers. Perfectionism has its place, but so does experimentation.

- **Respond.** Customer connections imply an ongoing dialogue between your brand and your customers. Don't drop your end of that conversation. For example, don't let social media queries and input go unanswered. These are your customers talking about your brand. Stay in the room and listen.

- **Learn.** If you're not testing something new, don't send the campaign out the door. Executives need to implement and enforce a learning agenda within their organizations to ensure that all marketing professionals are committed to brand evolution. If you're not changing, you're standing still. And that makes you vulnerable to the competition.

- **Be consistent, but flexible.** You may need to use different metrics and measures in some cases. But always have a common metric that keeps your marketing on course.

Use Technology to Enable, Not Distract

Technology often seems like a panacea to what ails the modern world, and marketing is no exception. Every new technology that enters the marketplace fires the imagination of marketers, who see it as a way to make marketing more effective—and ideally, to make their work less stressful. But technology is only an enabler of change, not the change itself.

Consider what you need for igniting and nurturing customer relationships, and then find the technology that makes it happen. Back in the day, we used to figure out what capabilities we needed first, and then we bought the computer that ran the right software. Technology can help you build strong customer relationships. Or it can do the opposite. It's all about what you do with it.

That said, the choices are almost endless, and trying to keep up can be daunting. Instead, look for the macro shifts, where tech companies are building and integrating. If you are a large company, look at what IBM, Oracle, Salesforce.com, Adobe, and of course my company, Epsilon, are doing to build the future of the marketing technology stack. They are doing some of the work to integrate content, channels, and data together. If you are a smaller company, there are also great tools. Companies like Constant Contact and HubSpot have brought easy-to-use sophistication to the marketplace. You can be sure there will be more and more capabilities, closer integration, and new possibilities—all enabled by customer data.

Make Your Transformation a Reality

Pursuing these four strategies requires more than technology, good ideas, or committed people. It requires rising above the details to look across your entire environment—and line up the people, process, and technology to create an efficient, effective, and fluid environment for planning and executing marketing. (See Figure 6.2.)

People, process, technology—each of these enabling elements is important. But the connections between them are critical, since they are all interconnected and need to move ahead consistently and in lock-step. It will not serve your organization well to go out and buy software or services without first developing a good strategy and identifying people who know how to use these new capabilities to get real results.

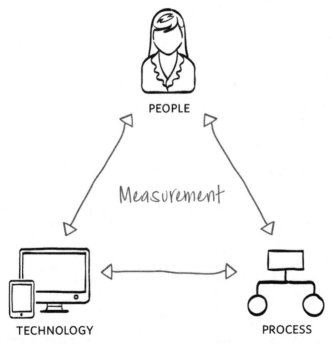

Figure 6.2 All three of these key elements have to work together to enable impressive marketing results.

In short, brilliant people with great ideas can get swallowed up by the process and technology intended to deploy those ideas. I've seen it happen over and over.

Think about engagement and experience and the parts of your company that can make the biggest impact. In my experience, they will include people, processes, and technology in most cases. Prioritize your efforts by looking at the enablers with the biggest impact. Keep these elements in balance, and constantly measure the end results—stronger customer connections. They are the true test of whether your transformation is working.

Loyalty Matters

Loyalty programs are on the rise, and with good reason. Identifying and rewarding your most loyal customers helps improve their experience with your brand, deepen their connection, and deliver brand and business equity. Loyalty programs also offer a great opportunity to connect directly with customers across channels, because the membership in the program persistently identifies them. Fueled by new technology, today's loyalty programs are dynamic, powerful, and important. In short, loyalty isn't just about miles or points anymore. It's about creating an incredibly strong bond with your best customers. Here are six strategies for building loyalty.

1. **Define what loyalty means for *your* company.** Loyalty means something different to every organization, a fact that look-alike programs fail to recognize. Explore and describe what loyalty means specifically to yours. Ensure that any

loyalty initiative matches your brand's personality and the needs of your customers—from the rewards you offer to the tone of all your communications.

2. **Give your customers the connection and appreciation they want.** It's not just about the big, high-ticket rewards. Make sure the reward or point of recognition is attainable and has a high perceived value by your consumers. It's about feeling recognized and rewarded with every interaction with your brand. Even small, incremental rewards (an upgrade, $5 off at point of sale) can delight and satisfy.

3. **Streamline your infrastructure to get seamless access to customer data.** To connect with customers, you have to know as much about them as possible. Too often, siloes keep data disconnected. Envision a *customer infrastructure*, where customer knowledge can be accessed, analyzed, updated, and more.

4. **Use your loyalty program to create connections across channels.** For companies, one of the great benefits of loyalty programs is that when consumers sign up they provide information about themselves. This information gives many companies the opportunity to see customer behavior that they would not normally see. For example, we all log into websites (often with an e-mail address) to see what deals we can get from a loyalty program. Loyalty allows brands to have access to vast information to deliver high-quality experiences.

5. **Keep customers engaged.** Ongoing engagement, not just episodic engagement, is at the heart of loyalty. Consider what to do during nonpurchase periods to keep loyalty

(continued)

members engaged with your brand. It's important not to let anyone fall off the radar.

6. **Use loyalty as a competitive weapon.** We live in an era of mature markets. Done right, loyalty is a way to differentiate your company—and hold on to your customers. Loyal customers are great advocates, making loyalty and engagement even more important.

Part Two
ROE² Research and Insights

Return on Experience × Engagement (ROE²) is an approach that transcends all industries and market segments, applies to companies of all sizes, and extends from business-to-business (B2B) to business-to-consumer (B2C) to B2B2C organizations. In this part of the book, we present quantitative evidence of the impact of ROE² drawn from research commissioned for this book, plus qualitative insights from executives with firsthand experience with ROE² within their organizations. The combination of data from tens of thousands of consumers, plus the perspectives of industry leaders, proves that ROE² is a powerful approach that benefits the marketing organizations that rely on it.

Chapter 7
Executive Insights: Dunkin' Donuts

How This Iconic American Brand Connects with Its Customers

We've positioned customer engagement as a critical element of Return on Experience × Engagement (ROE^2)—the actions that consumers take that end up delivering business equity, a slightly more complicated way of describing a more bottom-line measurement: actions that drive sales. Now we'll take a look at how customer engagement and experience play out at one of the best-known and best-loved brands in the United States, Dunkin' Donuts. I interviewed John Costello, President of Global Marketing and Innovation at Dunkin' Donuts and an early pioneer of

John Costello, President, Global Marketing and Innovation, Dunkin' Brands, Inc.

omnichannel marketing. Our discussion focused on Dunkin' Donuts' very successful work transitioning to more digital channels and using innovative initiatives to drive real gains in brand and business equity. Here are some of the highlights of our interview.

* * *

Andy Frawley: Tell us a bit about how Dunkin' Donuts has transitioned from mass marketing to digital channels and the impact it has had on how you think about experience and engagement.

John Costello: For many years, mass marketing was the most effective and efficient way to build our brand and drive sales. One-to-one marketing was more measurable and direct, but it didn't have the scale and immediacy of mass marketing. What we're seeing is that consumer engagement is changing around the world. We used to reach a high percentage of consumers quickly and effectively by buying media in a small number of channels—mainly TV and outdoor venues. Trends in consumer engagement are changing the way consumers want to get information from brands.

Now consumers want to get information when they want it, where they want it, and how they want it. They have more devices and more distractions. They've moved into a multiscreen world—with more consumers getting information from multiple screens, often concurrently.

At Dunkin' Donuts, our traditional marketing and media still work very effectively for us. But we're moving to an omnichannel approach to communicate with customers.

Andy Frawley: How does this affect their experience with your brand?

John Costello: I believe that everything that touches the consumer defines their experience. So it's very important to engage customers where and when they are now, and that requires omnichannel outreach. Traditional mass media and marketing are still effective for us, and they're not going away. But digital marketing is growing at a faster rate.

Andy Frawley: How do you keep the customer experience consistent with so many channels?

John Costello: It's important to integrate across all of the consumer touch points. In our case, we're making sure that all our communications are relevant to the medium in which they run, as well as consistent. As a result, our mobile, digital, social, TV, and print messaging is all very consistent.

Andy Frawley: What makes a strong customer connection?

John Costello: What I've found over the past 20 years is that the tactics have changed, but the fundamental principles have not. The most important factor in building a strong customer connection is making sure that you understand your customers' unmet needs better than anyone else. And ensure that you deliver on those needs better than other choices. Brand differentiation is more important that it's ever been. As people explore new channels, your message to them should still answer the most important question—*Why should the consumer choose your brand over a wealth of other choices?*

Andy Frawley: Are all channels created equal?

John Costello: No. You have to make sure that your communication is consistent, of course. But you also have to recognize the unique nature of each channel. I think of TV as a *lean back* channel—consumers just lean back and get the messaging. Interactions with mobile devices and laptops are more *lean in* communications —they're much more personal. And social marketing is more about having a meaningful dialogue, and providing value to every interaction.

Andy Frawley: How is Dunkin' Donuts combining traditional and digital channels?

John Costello: Mass marketing is still very effective, but our digital connections are more important than ever. And we're moving to an omnichannel approach with mobile front and center. We see a real synergy in integrating traditional and digital marketing. We're searching for new ways to extend the emotional connection and powerful customer experiences that drive customer engagement and result in purchases. And that means connecting old and new approaches.

Andy Frawley: Can you give us an example?

John Costello: Sure, we have a relationship with the television show *Top Chef*. And as part of one of the seasons, Dunkin' Donuts coffee was one of the mystery ingredients that the chefs had to use when making up recipes. In parallel, we set up a Google hangout and invited people to create their own recipes with our coffee. Our chefs in the Dunkin' Brands test kitchen recreated some of the recipes that people submitted, and our executive chef picked the winner. So that's an example of how we inspired real-time sharing of passion for Dunkin' Donuts coffee via a traditional sponsorship of a TV program and also extended to include a powerful online component on Google+.

Here's another. We purchased a billboard in Times Square in New York and recently converted it to 100 percent digital. Our customers post a Facebook photo of themselves and we select a different fan each week to be Fan of the Week (FotW), then we post their image on the billboard for the entire week.

Andy Frawley: What about mobile?

John Costello: Here's an interesting one. We've been strengthening and expanding our DD Perks® loyalty program, which we use to reward loyal guests and encourage them to visit multiple times during the day. While traditional marketing remains very effective for Dunkin' Donuts, we believe that DD Perks will be a major driver of business in the future. In new markets, we use mobile to create local customers using the one-to-one aspect of mobile plus loyalty.

And there are many ways to get people to download the mobile app. We have ties to lots of local professional sports teams (the New England Patriots, Philadelphia Eagles, New York Yankees, New York Mets, Atlanta Braves, and Miami Heat, etc.). In those markets we did a mobile promotion that rewarded people who downloaded the mobile app with a free cup of coffee—only if the local team won a specified game. That's a great, integrated program that ties together sports marketing, mobile, and loyalty.

Andy Frawley: How else are you using the DD Perks loyalty program to build customer connections?

John Costello: We launched the mobile app in August 2011 and expanded it in January 2014. And we've experienced rapid adoption. The one-to-one marketing aspects of our DD Perks program and mobile app enable us to test much broader ways of engaging with consumers. We can see what messaging and offers provide the most value and get the best response. We can provide consistently powerful communications across our entire customer base, but also grow profitable sales for our local franchises.

Andy Frawley: It's clear that Dunkin' Donuts isn't shy about adopting technology and experimenting with it to build your brand. Talk a bit about other technology initiatives.

John Costello: I think that Big Data offers huge opportunities to understand the customer and what's working or not. But Big Data by itself isn't a strategy. Big Data can help you build an advantage and make you more competitive. But it supplements your judgment; it doesn't replace it. The most effective way to use it is to focus on the questions that you want answered and use Big Data to answer them—not just gather lots of data for data's sake. It's an enabler, not a strategy. And that holds true for a lot of emerging technologies and tools.

Andy Frawley: What about measurement?

John Costello: There's been a lot of progress on improving how we measure ROI for traditional marketing, and also digital tools. But there's a lot of work that needs to be done to help measure the relationship between engagement, brand building, and sales, as well as measuring and attributing engagement driven by some of the newer social media.

Andy Frawley: Any final words on inspiring customer connections?

John Costello: The rapid adoption of digital and mobile technology has enabled a more direct connection with consumers. And it's really accelerated our ability to create and measure the impact of our marketing better than ever before. We're both a strong national brand and a very local collection of franchises. So our mobile and loyalty efforts can balance national, regional, and local programs, balancing the immediacy of one-on-one customer engagement while getting the economies of scale of regional and national marketing. We're combining traditional marketing, digital marketing, mobile, social, loyalty marketing, advanced measurement, and more. And it's definitely working.

Executive Insights — Dunkin' Donuts

- Content is key to driving Engagement × Experience. It's important to link and leverage content across channels.

- Mobile is key, since it keeps the customers connected everywhere.

- Big Data is an important enabler, but does not drive results by itself.

Chapter 8
ROE^2 in the Grocery Aisles

How Do Emotion and Experience Influence Grocery Consumers?

Extensive research in the grocery category, conducted exclusively for *Igniting Customer Connections*, shows the role of emotions, one of the key elements of experience, in consumer purchase behavior—and uncovers insights that stretch far beyond the category. As we established in our initial discussion of Return on Experience × Engagement (ROE^2), the customers' emotional experience—*how they feel*—is a key factor in driving business outcomes, such as brand commitment and share of wallet (the two measures of ROE^2 in this research). And here we see that hypothesis proven by the data.

* * *

Many people think that customers make buying decisions based solely on a rational approach, analyzing details like price and convenience. In fact, emotions play a larger role in shaping purchase behavior and, more specifically, strengthening the emotional connection to a brand. This trend, as we discovered, is particularly evident in the grocery category.

Grocery competition used to be about convenience and selection. Now it's about branding. Some stores (Whole Foods, Trader Joe's, and many more) have transformed what was once considered a boring chore into a memorable destination experience. The result is that many consumers are now committed to a specific grocery brand because they expect to be entertained and have a unique experience.

The Link between Emotion and Experience

Most customer-centric marketing strategies are designed to increase customer engagement. The premise is that more relevant interactions with customers result in more transactions for the business. The problem is that meaningful experience requires emotional connection.

In a world of increasingly commoditized products and service-based brands, emotion (a key element of experience) is a tangible differentiator responsible for igniting connection and delivering sustainable business outcomes. Emotions drive experience, and experience drives behaviors—and the results of those behaviors can be evaluated and integrated into brand strategies. An ability to measure and manage deep emotional relationships with consumers over time is what will determine success in today's economy.

In an effort to quantify the most important drivers of business outcomes, we analyzed thousands of data points about adult consumers and linked their emotional and rational responses to various measures of brand and business equity.

The key finding? We found that emotion (or in ROE² language, a primary element of customer experience) pays—by driving positive business outcomes. Here are some of the specific findings that back it up.

A Personal, Emotional Connection Matters

If a brand fails to make an emotional connection with its customers, then their satisfaction scores are a misleading measure of performance.

While customer satisfaction is an important diagnostic to track, it is an insufficient measure of brand and business equity.

Generally, most consumers expressed satisfaction with most of the grocers rated—a common trend in a mature, commoditized category. With elevated levels of satisfaction, it's necessary to look deeper for attributes that distinguish brand identity and influence business outcomes.

As shown in Figure 8.1, highly satisfied responders with *low* emotional connection to the brand had business outcomes that were similar to those of the general pool of responders. However, highly satisfied responders with *high* emotional connection to the brand had significantly higher business outcomes across all measures of business and brand equity. Considering the top- and bottom-line impact of a 78 percent lift in share of wallet attributable to high emotional connection, it pays for brands to develop a deep understanding of emotional drivers.

Impact of Emotion on Business Outcomes

			Highly Satisfied		
Business Outcome	(scale)	All Responders	Low Emotion	High Emotion	% Lift*
Share of Wallet	(%)	21.8	23.6	42.2	+78%
Brand Commitment	(1-10)	5.9	6.2	8.2	+32%
Likelihood to Recommend	(1-10)	7.9	8.9	9.9	+11%
Purchase Intent	(1-5)	4.2	4.5	4.9	+9%

Figure 8.1 Satisfied customers aren't committed to the brand until they experience an emotional connection. This crucial point shows the power of ROE^2 as a catalyst.

* % Lift = (High Emotion − Low Emotion)/Low Emotion

Emotion Pays

If highly satisfied customers lacking an emotional connection with the brand are on par with the average customer, it prompts the question: which has more of an impact on business outcomes—emotion or logic/reason?

To explore this question, we modeled the relative impact of more than 100 emotions, cognitions, and brand perceptions on a broad range of business outcomes, including brand commitment, advocacy, share of wallet, and purchase intent. Several high-impact variables emerged as strong predictors of both brand and business equity.

Of the 14 model variables, the following three stood out as the top predictors of *all* business outcomes in the grocery category:

1. Total Number of Emotional Connections

Trust	A Connection
Liking	Warm
Interesting	Happy
Satisfied	Self-confident
Pleasure	Inspired

2. Total Number of Personal Attributes

Interesting	Down-to-earth
Successful	Easygoing
Competent	Likable
Reliable	Cool
Your kind of person	

3. Trust

In other words, brand preference is more a function of *feelings* than practical considerations. We conclude from our research that emotional connection is far more important than logical cognitions (such as price, convenience, service, or selection) in explaining a consumer's commitment to a particular brand. (See Figure 8.2.)

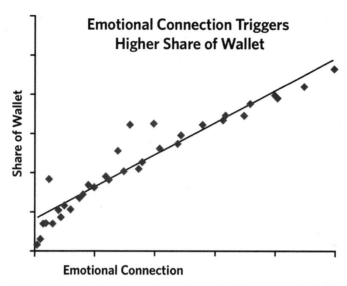

Figure 8.2 We ranked each customer based on the strength of his or her emotional connection with a particular brand. Then we plotted the share of wallet associated with that brand to quantify the value of the emotional connection.

This discovery highlights a potentially untapped opportunity for marketers to align brand positioning with personal values and needs. The ability of organizations to identify and address the specific emotional attributes and purchase drivers associated with their brands represents a distinct competitive advantage that can result in long-term growth and success.

More Trust Means More Share of Wallet and Brand Commitment

Consumers choose brands that align with their personal values and aspirations. It's the alignment of those values between the consumer and brand that ignites a meaningful connection, resulting in trust. And trust is a critical element of how a consumer experiences a brand.

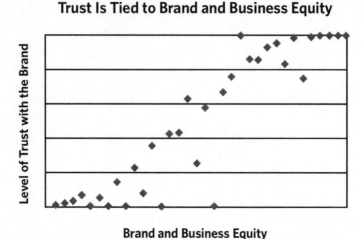

Figure 8.3   The plot of trust relative to measures of brand and business equity shows the strength of the relationship between these key elements.

Relationships are built on trust, and the research shows that business returns are built the same way. Once trust is established—often by delivering a consistently positive experience—favorable brand perceptions are created. Purchases happen with or without emotional connection. But transacting is a choice and, as Figure 8.3 illustrates, people choose to spend their money with brands they trust.

Emotions Can Outweigh Logical Reasoning

In *The Happiness Hypothesis* (Basic Books, 2006), Jonathan Haidt suggests that our emotional side is like an elephant and our rational side is like a rider perched atop the elephant. They work well together in tandem as long as the elephant and rider agree. When they disagree, the rider loses the ability to control the elephant.

Choosing which brand to purchase is the result of a combination of rational factors (price, convenience, service, selection) and emotional factors (trust, emotion, inspiration, stimulation). But what happens when there's an imbalance between the two? Our research shows that

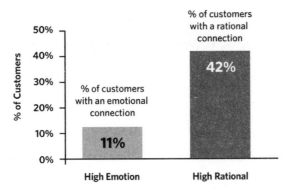

Figure 8.4   Of those customers reporting a high emotional connection with the brand, only 11 percent identified one or more rational considerations as important. Conversely, 42 percent of customers with a high rational connection to the brand listed one or more emotions as important.

even when rational factors outweigh emotions, emotions continue to be important contributors in the decision-making process. However, when emotional connections are high, they all but eliminate the influence of logical reasoning. In effect, the elephant is in control (see Figure 8.4).

The important implication is that a strong emotional connection will result in increased retention since committed customers are less likely to be tempted by lower prices from competitors (or other rational considerations). It also suggests that a miscue in the relationship could have immediate negative consequences.

More Emotional Connections = More Equity

The most important driver of brand and business equity is the total number of emotional connections between the brand and the customer. As shown in Figure 8.5, customers who report high brand and business equity average more than nine distinct emotional connections with the brand. Conversely, customers with low brand and business equity average less than one emotional connection.

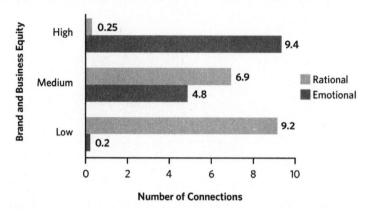

Figure 8.5 Brand and business equity increases as the number of emotional connections increases. The inverse is true for rational connections.

By listening to customers through vehicles such as surveys and social media, marketers can create meaningful experiences that resonate with a full range of emotions.

Common Ground at the Extremes

Until now, we've focused on some of the significant emotional and cognitive differences between consumer relationships. However, there are some similarities at the extremes that are just as interesting. For instance, the research shows no meaningful connection between business and brand equity and a customer's income (or age). (See Figure 8.6.) This finding underscores the limitations of traditional segmentation variables, such as age and income, in providing meaningful differentiation among customers.

Price versus Emotion

Brands are increasingly being forced to select one of two positions: discount brand with low emotional connection and premium brand with high emotional connection (or positive customer experience).

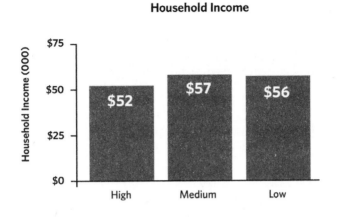

Figure 8.6 Business outcomes were consistent across key profile characteristics, such as age and household income.

A comparison of specific brands further demonstrates the impact emotional connection has on brand and business equity. (See Figure 8.7.) Grocery brands that place an emphasis on convenience and low prices (No Frills, Foodland, Save-On-Foods) have

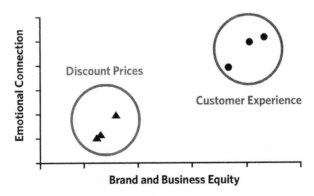

Figure 8.7 Brands with strong customer-oriented marketing programs generate positive experiences that result in emotional connection and (ultimately) sustained brand and business equity.

lower emotional connection and associated brand and business equity. Conversely, grocery brands dedicated to building relationships through customer experience and rewards programs (Sobeys, IGA, Safeway) have higher emotional connection and brand and business equity.

Emotion and Experience as Differentiators

As a new profit driver, emotional connection has a measurable and meaningful impact. Its reach is also universal—impacting all measures of business outcomes, including customer satisfaction, net promoter score, and share of wallet. Emotional connection represents a powerful form of differentiation in today's crowded and competitive marketing arena. Brands that succeed in establishing *true* connection with consumers will achieve a sustainable competitive advantage.

Chapter 9
Executive Insights: JCPenney

How JCPenney Uses Loyalty to Inspire Engagement

J CPenney is one of the nation's largest apparel and home furnishing retailers, with approximately 1,100 stores and online shopping via jcp.com. Although it is one of the most venerable brands in the United States, JCPenney is looking forward and embracing new technologies to focus on improving the customer brand experience. As part of this effort, JCPenney's leaders are integrating customer data, supporting customer communications across multiple channels, and creating a more engaging online platform for customer interactions. Much of this work focuses on transforming JCP Rewards, the company's member loyalty program. I spoke recently with Elmer Smith, Vice President of Customer

Elmer Smith, Vice President of Customer Strategy, JCPenney

Strategy at JCPenney, who is spearheading many of the company's customer-focused efforts.

* * *

Andy Frawley: What are some of the challenges that JCPenney faces?

Elmer Smith: Well, when I arrived in late 2012 we were a case study that proved how making important decisions without customer data will eventually kill you. Our previous actions had radically altered the focus of the company and sent our core customers fleeing. From a technical standpoint, we didn't have a 360-degree view of our customers. We had rewards program data, but it was disconnected from our core customer data, and online data was barely feeding into it at all. Our internal customer database wasn't very functional. We were really operating in a 1980s infrastructure and mind-set.

My first step was to focus on JCPenney Rewards, since a loyalty program identifies your best and most important customers. Those were the customers we wanted to keep and nurture. And once we knew more about them from their data, we could begin doing robust customer segmentation, developing divisional plans, and executing against them. But first, we had to transform our member loyalty program—and attract new members, too.

Andy Frawley: Give us an idea of the scope of JCPenney Rewards.

Elmer Smith: We have more than 42 million distinct JCPenney Rewards members and approximately 45 percent of our sales roll through the program.

Andy Frawley: We worked closely with you to provide more—and more detailed and accessible—data about your JCPenney Rewards members. What did that data do for you?

Elmer Smith: Understanding these core customers is critical to our future. Expanding and deepening our customer rewards program is a big initiative for us, one that will drive additional revenue and profitability. With more data, we can understand more about what specific customer groups want, and how they want to interact with us. For example, some JCPenney Rewards members like to get digital promotions but shop at the store. Others want to buy all online. And some are omnichannel customers. This information helps us get the *right message to them at the right time via the right channel,* and ultimately achieve a true one-to-one dialogue with millions of customers.

Andy Frawley: How did you expand the number of members in the program?

Elmer Smith: It's all part of our effort to improve the point-of-sale experience. Store execution is the key element. We did a lot of training to help store associates engage with customers, looking them up at point of sale, and inspiring them to be more active members of the program—or to join if they weren't members already. And it worked. We're signing up significantly more new members every month.

Andy Frawley: How does your rewards program inspire a better customer experience and engagement?

Elmer Smith: What we're trying to do is to tie in rewards with all of our marketing communications. We've created new levels of membership. And we personalize communication based on where they are in the program. After all, the whole point of the sales experience is to generate a conversation around loyalty. In the past, no one was talking about it, since they didn't have the data on the customer at the point of sale or at the call centers.

After all, increasing engagement with your customers is a by-product of being more relevant and personal. It's about understanding their needs and focusing all your efforts and tying them together in a cohesive way to meet those needs. Then they'll engage.

Andy Frawley: JCPenney is a very big company. How do you tie it all together?

Elmer Smith: We work to be relevant and consistent across all our channels. After all, our omnichannel customers are some of our best customers. In fact, we've seen that they contribute three times the value of other customers. Of our customer groups we have two main omnichannel groups that we need to retain and reactivate, and we're leveraging JCPenney Rewards heavily to get that done. We're focusing on delivering a compelling, consistent experience to these key groups. And technology is the foundation of everything that we do.

Andy Frawley: Tell us more about your data strategy.

Elmer Smith: First, we needed to get all our critical data in one place—a reliable, state-of-the-art customer data warehouse. We needed to bring the loyalty data into that warehouse as well. And we had to integrate all our digital channels as well. These are just fundamental steps that bring our core data together. Otherwise, unstructured data, Big Data—all of that is impossible.

It all starts with data. Data leads to insights, which lead to action. But you have to have the right data first. You can have the best analytics and analysts, but without clean core data, and lots of it, you're not going to get the job done.

Andy Frawley: How has your updated technological foundation enabled you to measure results?

Elmer Smith: Now we have campaign-level reporting, customer life-cycle reporting, reporting and analysis aligned with our customer segmentation, and multichannel reporting—capabilities that were unheard-of a few years ago. We're also using our customer data to fuel a robust, multichannel attribution project. Through these initiatives and other existing capabilities, we will be able to be much more efficient with our market spend because we will know more about which groups we want to reach and how they engage with our marketing communications. We'll know each customer's path to purchase, which will lead to higher (and more efficient) conversions. We're looking at customer lifetime value, and then using what we learn to bring in the right long-term customers, the kind who will fuel the growth of our company for years to come.

Executive Insights – JCPenney

- Loyalty programs are a great way to impact the experience a brand has with its consumers by providing different types and levels of rewards.

- A consistent data strategy is the basis of ROE^2. Without a data strategy it's impossible to drive Engagement × Experience.

- Omnichannel customers (highly engaged) are three times more valuable than standard customers. Delivering a consistent and effective experience is key.

Chapter **10**

ROE² in Hospitality

How Does Experience Impact How Consumers Choose Hotels?

E psilon conducted research to uncover which types of connections drive business outcomes in the hospitality industry. We analyzed thousands of data points for more than 3,000 adult personal and business travelers and asked them to identify their most frequent brand of hotel. Then, we identified and ranked the factors most closely associated with brand commitment and share-of-wallet intent.

We found that meaningful interactions and experiences ignite emotional connection with the brand, and this translates into profits. Consumers are looking for a connection, and they often find it when brands align with their self-image and personal values. As we'll see, these connections can be deeply personal and highly profitable.

Experience Impacts Business Outcomes

Each customer experience produces emotions that have a positive or negative effect on business outcomes. There's a point at which a positive (or negative) experience is so strong that it transcends the rational aspects of the brand (e.g., quality, price, service) and becomes a part of the brand itself. That's why creating and controlling the customer experience are so important.

Our research showed that while most respondents had a favorable impression of a brand's quality, ease, and service, the disparity between high- and low-emotion respondents was quite significant. (See Figure 10.1.)

High-emotion respondents had exceptionally favorable ratings of their primary brand's quality, ease, and service—suggesting that these rational drivers spark emotional attachment to the brand. An engaging experience leads to emotion, and as we'll see, emotion paves the way for increased brand and business equity.

Emotion Matters

	"Do you agree with the following…"	All Responders	Low Emotion	High Emotion	% Lift*
QUALITY	Properties are well maintained	72%	46%	97%	+109%
	Guest rooms are well maintained	71%	47%	95%	+100%
	High-quality bed/pillows	70%	45%	95%	+113%
EASE	Check-in process is efficient	75%	53%	95%	+78%
	Booking a stay is easy	73%	52%	93%	+78%
SERVICE	Staff is friendly	73%	52%	94%	+81%
	Staff is responsive	70%	47%	93%	+97%
	Staff resolves problems quickly	56%	36%	83%	+127%

Figure 10.1 Customers rated 24 positive experiential attributes on a scale of 1 (completely disagree) to 5 (completely agree). Customers who completely agreed with 17 or more attributes were classified as high-emotion customers. Low-emotion customers completely agreed with 0 attributes.

* % Lift = (High Emotion − Low Emotion)/Low Emotion.

Experience Creates Emotion, and Emotion Fuels Engagement

Managing experience across every interaction in the customer journey is critical because a customer's experience with your brand is the primary driver of perception and action. And there's a positive relationship between actions and transactions. Our research shows that when experience ignites emotion, a customer is more eager to interact and more willing to spend money with a brand. (See Figure 10.2.)

Simply put, happy customers are eager to interact and more willing to spend money with their favorite brands. But it doesn't end there.

Emotion serves as an accelerant, spreading positive and negative experiences to the masses via word of mouth and online testimonials. And those with the highest emotional connection tend to speak the loudest. Our research showed that high-emotion respondents were

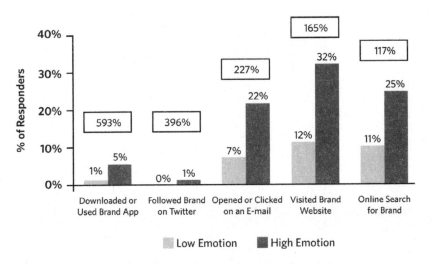

Figure 10.2 An emotional connection triggers action.

Caring Drives Sharing

"In the past three months, which of the following have you done…"	All Responders	Low Emotion	High Emotion	% Lift*
Bought something from the brand	2%	0%	4%	+2,233%
Liked/visited the brand on Facebook	3%	1%	4%	+692%
Offered praise to the brand	14%	4%	27%	+548%
Talked about the brand with others	19%	7%	35%	+392%
Posted a review online for the brand	4%	2%	7%	+360%
Responded to a brand survey	13%	7%	20%	+202%

Figure 10.3   An emotional connection with a brand helps inspire sharing.

* % Lift = (High Emotion − Low Emotion)/Low Emotion.

significantly more likely than low-emotion respondents to share their feelings about brand experiences.

An emotionally engaging experience begins with a positive interaction. The more positive interactions a brand can deliver, the greater its chances of reaching the tipping point where emotion becomes part of the brand.

The Connection between Experience, Emotion, and Engagement

Experience creates emotion, and emotion is what makes an engagement meaningful. In fact, our research revealed that in the absence of an emotional connection, highly engaged customers provide no incremental benefit to business outcomes. (See Figure 10.4.)

However, the pace at which customers increase their future share is dramatically increased when there's an emotional connection. For

Impact on Business Outcomes

Business Outcome	(Scale)	All Responders	Highly Engaged		
			Low Emotion	High Emotion	% Lift*
Increase Future Share	(%)	16%	16%	32%	+100%
Brand Commitment	(1–6)	4.4	4.0	5.3	+32%
Likelihood to Recommend	(1–10)	8.4	7.3	9.8	+34%
Likelihood to stay on Next Trip	(1–5)	3.9	3.6	4.6	+27%

Figure 10.4 Highly engaged customers are those with five or more brand interactions in the most recent three months. Coupled with a high emotional connection, these customers bring significant impact to business outcomes.

* % Lift = (High Emotion – Low Emotion)/Low Emotion.

instance, highly engaged, high-emotion customers were *twice* as likely (32 percent) as highly engaged, low-emotion customers (16 percent) to report that they intended to increase their future share with their most frequented brand of hotel. By contrast, there was no difference between highly engaged, low-emotion customers and the average respondent regarding future intent. The same holds true for brand commitment, likelihood to recommend, and likelihood to return. What this tells us is that engagement derives much of its value from the emotion created by a positive experience.

Through modeling, we identified several factors that not only were statistically linked to business outcomes in the hospitality industry, but were ultimately responsible for driving those outcomes. Each factor was then ranked according to its influence on brand commitment and share-of-wallet intent—the brand equity and business equity

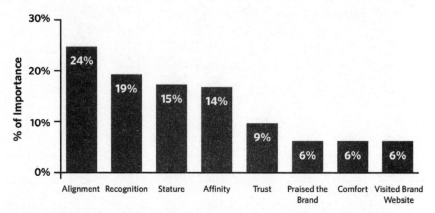

Figure 10.5   Our predictive model identified eight factors contributing to ROE². The most influential factor was alignment, which explained 24 percent of the change in ROE².

components, respectively, of Return on Experience × Engagement (ROE²). (See Figure 10.5.)

Specifically, the following three key drivers collectively had overwhelming influence on brand and business equity.

1. *Alignment* with Image and Personal Values

   ◆ This is a hotel for someone like me.

   ◆ It says a lot about me.

   ◆ It fits my lifestyle.

   ◆ This hotel treats me as an individual.

   ◆ It has values consistent with mine.

   ◆ This hotel and I are a perfect fit.

   ◆ It fulfills my needs better than other hotels do.

2. *Recognition* for Loyalty

   ◆ I can earn points with the hotel and my credit card.

   ◆ I can earn bonus points.

- ◆ I can stay on points.
- ◆ The hotel offers other favorable points options.

3. *Perception* of Stature

- ◆ This hotel has a good reputation.
- ◆ It is a highly respected name in hotels.
- ◆ It is a hotel I consider to be a leader in the category.

Once the drivers of business outcomes are identified—and the influence each contributes to the relationship with the customer is understood—it's possible to design and deliver an emotionally engaging experience tied to top- and bottom-line growth.

It all starts with alignment.

Key Driver #1: *Alignment* with Image and Personal Values

Consumers seek out brands that reflect their self-image and align with their personal values. (See Figure 10.6.) This alignment of image and values ignites an emotional connection. When consumers can relate to a brand, they are more open to developing an enduring relationship.

Nearly all of the high-emotion respondents indicated that they choose a hotel brand that has values consistent with their own. (See Figure 10.7.) This finding not only demonstrates the significance of value alignment, but also shows the importance of a brand making its values known to the consumer. We'll explore the critical importance of content in Part Three.

By contrast, only 38 percent of consumers with a low emotional connection to the brand indicated that the brand shared their values. The difference in value alignment between low- and high-emotion consumers translated into an ROE² (share-of-wallet intent and brand commitment) that was 389 percent higher for the emotionally connected consumer.

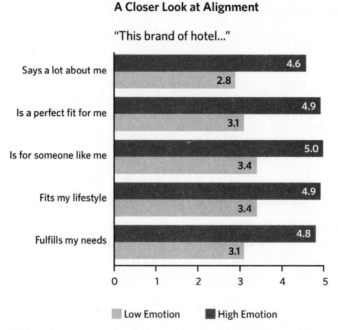

A Closer Look at Alignment

"This brand of hotel..."

Low Emotion   High Emotion

Figure 10.6 On a scale of 1 to 5, with 1 being "completely disagree" and 5 being "completely agree," customers expressing a high emotional connection with their most frequented hotel brand averaged 4.6 or better.

While values like trust skewed toward high-emotion consumers, low-emotion respondents focused on more rational characteristics, such as hotel rate, proximity, and amenities (like free breakfast).

The significance of these findings is that in the absence of an emotional connection, consumers are more heavily influenced by cognitive factors when making brand choices. Not surprisingly, these consumers are also much more likely to consider alternative brands. (See Figure 10.8.) We'll explore issues related to measurement and segmentation in Part Three.

Key Driver #2: *Recognition* for Loyalty

Despite a steady increase in loyalty membership across all industries in recent years, loyalty programs often fail to deliver profitable returns

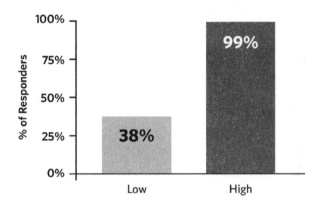

Core Values Matter

"This brand of hotel has values consistent with mine"

Figure 10.7 Consumers prefer to do business with brands that reflect their core values and beliefs.

Connection Generates Continuity

"I stay at this brand of hotel for **every trip**—whether I am paying or my company is paying."

Emotional Connection	% of Responders
High	42%
Low	6%

Figure 10.8 Emotionally connected consumers become repeat customers.

for a number of reasons—including high program costs and a failure to target those customers responsible for driving profits. However, our research shows that not only are loyalty programs in the hospitality sector effective at creating emotional connection, but they're also responsible for helping to deliver improvements in brand and business equity. (See Figure 10.9.)

In our modeling, the relationship between loyalty rewards and brand and business equity was both positive and profound. For instance, more than one-half of high-ROE^2 respondents indicated that their reason for choosing a particular brand of hotel was influenced by the ability to earn bonus points. By contrast, only 4 percent of low-ROE^2 respondents cited bonus points as a factor when choosing a hotel.

Customers like to be recognized for their patronage, and when that recognition comes from a brand they can relate to, it serves to reinforce the emotional connection.

Loyalty Improves Brand and Business Equity

"Why did you choose this hotel?"	All Responders	Low Brand/Business Equity	High Brand/Business Equity	% Lift*
I can earn points with the hotel and my credit card	15%	2%	34%	+1,418%
I can earn bonus points	25%	4%	52%	+1,327%
I can stay on points	18%	3%	40%	+1,071%
Offers other favorable points options	9%	4%	17%	+363%

Figure 10.9 Each respondent received a model score based on his or her brand commitment and share-of-wallet intent information. We used the resulting scores to rank and classify customers into high, medium, or low brand and business equity customers.

* % Lift = (High Brand/Business Equity – Low Brand/Business Equity)/Low Brand/Business Equity.

Key Driver #3: *Perception* of Stature

A brand's stature is an intangible asset derived from perception, and it can be reinforced or destroyed by emotional experience.

Our research found that the perception of a brand as a leader and respected name in the hospitality category not only had a significant positive impact, but was also related to a consumer's emotional connection with the brand. Those with the highest emotional connection also had the most favorable impression of the brand's stature. (See Figure 10.10.)

Reputation also has a powerful influence on consumer choice and both affects and is affected by emotional connections. When a consumer has a positive impression of a brand and feels that the brand says a lot about the consumer as a person, the resulting bond is difficult for competitors to break.

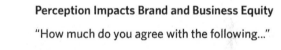

Perception Impacts Brand and Business Equity

"How much do you agree with the following..."

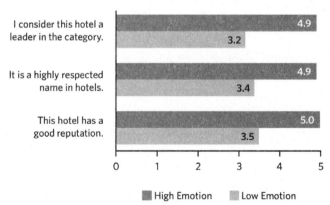

Figure 10.10   On a scale of 1 to 5, with 5 being "completely agree," customers expressing a high emotional connection with their most frequented hotel brand averaged 4.9 or better.

Customer Experience: Creating the Highest Levels of Brand and Business Equity

In an industry heavily dependent on brand loyalty and repeat business, it's no surprise that brands devoted to customer satisfaction and experience—such as Disney, Marriott, and Hilton—have the highest levels of customer engagement, emotional connection, and brand and business equity. (See Figure 10.11.)

Brands with the highest associated ROE² in our survey share a philosophy deep-rooted in customer service, and their customer-centric approach has resulted in deep, emotional connections and meaningful engagements with their customers. For instance, Marriott customers reported 53 percent more positive experiences with the brand than

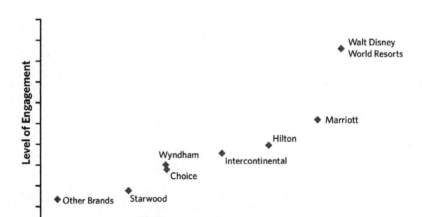

Figure 10.11   Respondents were asked to identify which interactions (from a list of 30) they've had with their most frequent hotel brand in the most recent three months. The more interactions a customer had with the brand, the higher the customer's commitment and share-of-wallet intent—the ultimate ROE².

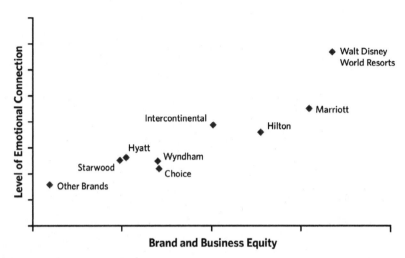

Figure 10.12 Emotional connection represents the number and strength of emotional attributes a respondent associated with his or her most frequent hotel brand. Brand commitment and share-of-wallet intent (brand and business equity) increase as a consumer's emotional connection with the brand increases.

Hyatt customers over a three-month period, and Marriott's corresponding ROE^2 was 63 percent higher, as shown in Figure 10.12.

Conversely, brands whose customers reported low levels of engagement and emotional connection tend to compete on price rather than customer experience, and price was not found to be an important determinant of brand and business equity. As a result, customers who frequent these brands are more likely to remain attentive to practical considerations (like price) that are often easily satisfied by competitors.

Long-Term Commitment: The Ultimate Goal

While it's important to track customer satisfaction, our research has shown that customer satisfaction is an insufficient measure of business and brand equity.

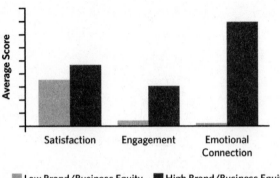

Figure 10.13 Customer satisfaction doesn't necessarily produce brand commitment or share-of-wallet intent. However, positive experiences and emotions, as well as meaningful engagements, yield better business outcomes.

Most customers were about equally satisfied with their brand experiences. (See Figure 10.13.) However, highly connected customers were far more engaged and much more emotionally linked with the brand than other customers were.

The most successful brands connect with customers on an emotional level by delivering a positive experience that aligns with the brand promise. Customers choose brands based on personal values, and once they've found a brand that reinforces their self-image they're more likely to make a long-term commitment. Marketers who succeed at developing personal, emotional connections with customers will realize a boost in brand and business equity.

Chapter 11
Executive Insights: Angie's List

Find Out How Angie's List Keeps Its Members Engaged with Its Brand

D elivering positive experiences to customers is a vital part of Return on Experience × Engagement (ROE²). And experience is at the core of Angie's List, the pioneering word-of-mouth network of more than three million households, where consumers share experiences to help find the best service companies and health care providers in their area. The company's tagline, *Reviews you can trust*, captures the concept at the heart of Angie's List: unbiased consumer accounts of members' experiences with service providers from painters to pediatricians. During the past few years, the company has expanded into ecommerce and created a private marketplace for members and top-rated service providers.

I interviewed Patrick Brady, President of Marketplace and Ecommerce at Angie's

Patrick Brady, President of Marketplace, Angie's List

List, about how his company delivers a great experience to its millions of members. Here are some of the key points we discussed.

* * *

Andy Frawley: How is Angie's List different from other organizations in terms of delivering a great consumer experience?

Patrick Brady: First and foremost, Angie's List is different because we balance people, process, and technology. We love technology, from elegant user interfaces to exceptional user experiences, but we go beyond technology. Our 2,000+ employees feel a moral and ethical obligation to solve our members' service needs. As our TV commercials say, "The app makes it easy, the power of Angie's List makes it work." The power of Angie's List comes from our employees, real people (not algorithms), who are armed with unparalleled data about service providers, and who are able to actually step in and help create happy service transaction outcomes.

We're also different because we are a paid membership model and a true, multi-party curated exchange, or private marketplace. Paid members expect more, and demand more, than simple registrants and casual consumers. Participants in a private exchange expect a higher level of service than in an open marketplace, so we had to design a system that could deliver a higher level of satisfaction—and at scale. Our members show their commitment to our brand right up front, when they pay to become paid-subscription members of Angie's List. In return, Angie's List sets a high bar for member satisfaction, since we must respect the member's commitment to our brand. Member value drives how we think about experience, interactions, engagement, and loyalty.

Finally, we are omnichannel, so we deliver great customer experience through many more channels than our competitors. We deliver our service through mobile, tablet, web, telephony, mail, incoming, outgoing—even directly to our members' front doors with a live rep. Moreover, we have to deliver great customer experience through hundreds of thousands of service providers. Our members expect more from these service providers, because they found them through us.

Andy Frawley: How does this model affect your interactions with members?

Patrick Brady: When you've paid to be a member of any group, like an affinity club or country club, your expectations are going to be higher because you feel like you're part owner of the organization. We treat our members like they're part of an exclusive club. And we really have to deliver the best possible interactions and experience to them. Under the membership model, we clearly serve the members and become their advocate, rather than just trying to sell them something.

Andy Frawley: What do your members want from their Angie's List experience?

Patrick Brady: *Happy transactions* and *remarkably superior service.* They want the fastest solution to their service needs with the least hassle. They want *Fair Price. Done Right. No Hassle.* They want service so much better than service procured without the help of Angie's List that they tell others about it. Our members want to search, shop, and SnapFix (our mobile app) their service needs away. Our members tend to be *do it for me* people—people who want to get the best possible services. They rely on us to help them make it happen. We have to deliver the capabilities that make the whole process as fast and easy as possible. After all, these are people who have more money than time. They want to get a problem solved right, quickly. Our job is to help them solve their problems in an extremely satisfying way. And every interaction we have with our members has to focus on solving their problems quickly.

We've always been thought of as the place to go for unbiased reviews you can trust. That's the way to ensure success with home services. But today we are much more than just a review site. We focus on the best way to get the problem solved. That's what our members want.

Andy Frawley: Describe the role of technology in delivering a great experience to Angie's List members.

Patrick Brady: We're using technology now in every aspect of the members' experience. They're not just going to a website to read reviews anymore. They're using their mobile devices to find what they need in seconds. With our SnapFix mobile app, our members can just snap a picture of a home problem—a leaky faucet or a broken fence—and hit *submit*. We will dispatch a top-rated service provider to solve their problem. We're using technology every way we can to accelerate our ability to serve our members, faster and better. That means mobile, Big Data, cloud— everything and anything that can give us an advantage and serve our members and service providers better.

Andy Frawley: How do you use data to improve the member experience?

Patrick Brady: We're a very data-centric company. Our challenge is to get better data and better knowledge, the kind that lets us really know our members. By knowing more about our members, we can serve them better. For example, when members call, they expect we're going to know what services they've used, how long they've been members, and lots more. Because they've paid to be members, they really do expect us to know a lot about them. And one of the good things about the membership model is that members are very vocal. They tell you what they want.

By gathering and analyzing data, we can ensure that our members are happy, and that we're continually meeting their needs. We do a lot of good old-fashioned outreach. And we do it continually via many channels—from responsive, knowledgeable customer service to our mobile app.

Andy Frawley: One of our key points is that experience really matters to consumers and that consumers who have great experiences and engage with a company end up delivering brand and business equity. Your model mirrors this concept, doesn't it?

Patrick Brady: It does. It's at the core of our brand. It's our DNA. We don't sell a product or a service. We sell an overall experience—what you experience from the time you realize you have a service need until that need is satisfied. That's your total member experience. The experience that members feel after they work with a service provider, let's say a plumber, is critical. We capture that experience in the form of member reviews and through a quantitative scoring system. We facilitate the correct match so our members get the most relevant result—the right plumber for the right plumbing problem, for example, so that the member can have a great experience. And if the experience is great, they'll choose to work with the plumber again and again—and recommend that plumber to others. So yes, it's experience that drives business equity for Angie's List, but it also drives value for the plumber. Our business is built around a huge collection of accumulated experiences, organized and curated and carefully controlled for quality and accuracy. In turn, we have to deliver a great experience to our members as they seek new service providers, take on new projects, solve problems, and live their lives.

Andy Frawley: Reviews are, ultimately, the content that your members are consuming, right?

Patrick Brady: Yes and no. Historically, unbiased member reviews comprised our main content, as well as great information from our publications. But we have also always been about delivering a superior service experience. It was the ultimate experience that our members were, and are, consuming. Today, our members are consuming reviews as content. But they are also consuming content in the form of technology-enabled quantitative scoring. So content is key to our members and service providers. We're at the intersection between these groups. And delivering the most compelling, helpful content in the form of performance reviews and results is one of the ways we provide value. We're constantly measuring service providers and helping them become better and stronger, and squeezing out inefficiency and waste—time *and* money—from the process.

Today, our members are also consuming pre-packaged services in our Shop channels, and are consuming solutions to their service problems in our SnapFix channels, in substantial and growing numbers.

Andy Frawley: What's changing in terms of providing value and delivering a great experience to your members?

Patrick Brady: The table stakes are higher. Members expect to be recognized instantly, no matter how they connect with us. The pace is faster. And we have to be continually raising our own bar on what it means to deliver *remarkably superior service*. The more we know about our members before they engage with us, the more remarkable we can make the experience. For example, if we know what types of systems they have in their house, like the specific brand and model of their furnace, we can ensure that a service technician they find through Angie's List has experience with that type of furnace. We can deliver a customized portfolio of service providers who know their systems, meet their needs, and charge the right price.

We do a lot for our members. But we're always looking for the next way we can do more for them—which means looking for new ways to make their experience with Angie's List fantastic every time they engage with us, project after project, year after year.

Executive Insights — Angie's List

- Experience is a critical determinant of whether Angie's List members will work with a service provider again.

- Delivering a great experience is even more critical when serving members who have paid to join.

- Gathering and analyzing member data on an ongoing basis help to deliver better experiences and deeper engagement.

- Omnichannel outreach is critical in connecting with Angie's List members and delivering the capabilities they want, quickly and easily.

Chapter 12
ROE^2 Hits the Road

What Drives Consumer Behavior When Buying a Car?

I f you thought that quality and value for the money were the leading influencers fueling car buying and servicing decisions, you would be wrong. When it comes to purchasing or servicing a vehicle, the reasons behind consumer behavior can't be explained by reason alone.

Whether driven by status, need, or simply a desire to drive, consumers love their automobiles. In fact, some of us go so far as to name our vehicles and grieve over the thought of trading them in someday. While car ownership might be a practical decision born out of necessity, the decisions behind what we buy and how we choose to care for our vehicle are deep-rooted in emotion, a critical element in the experience side of Return on Experience × Engagement (ROE^2).

As our research of the grocery industry demonstrated in Chapter 8, emotion is a powerful brand differentiator that has a profound impact on consumer decisions. If a mundane activity like shopping for food can be propelled by an undercurrent of feelings, then it stands to reason that an industry predicated on uniting consumers with the freedom of the road would also find success in making an emotional connection with the consumer.

What Drives Consumer Behavior?

Since car ownership is one of the costliest relationships we enter into during our lifetimes, we wanted to know if emotional factors overshadow functional considerations when choosing a brand or service location. We also wanted to see if the same emotional connections and meaningful experiences that influence the purchase of a vehicle also contribute to where we choose to service our vehicle.

We surveyed nearly 4,000 vehicle owners with a comprehensive series of cognitive and emotional questions regarding the experiences and engagements they've had with the manufacturer of their automobile and the dealership where they most frequently have their vehicle serviced. We then built predictive models to link survey responses to measures of business and brand equity. For the purpose of this analysis we selected repurchase intent and commitment to the dealership (for service) as the two most meaningful business outcomes.

We found that consumers repurchase from trustworthy brands that align with their personal values, and they have their vehicle serviced at the dealership if they respect and trust the staff. While not necessarily a surprise, the absence of functional considerations—such as quality and price—as key drivers was noteworthy.

What *did* surprise us was that our feelings about the brand influence where we choose to have our vehicle serviced, and our experiences with the dealership strengthen (or diminish) our perception of the brand. When we quantified the business impact of these meaningful experiences and engagements, we discovered that the result wasn't linear—it was exponential.

Functionality Doesn't Motivate

Generally speaking, people buy for emotional reasons and fall back on logic to rationalize their choices. We might tout gas mileage, resale

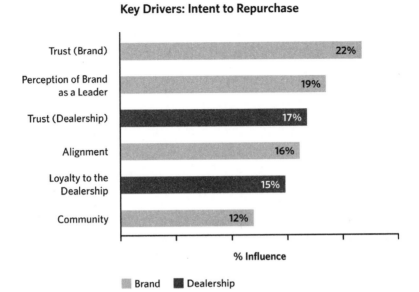

Figure 12.1   Intent to repurchase from the manufacturer is a function of four brand factors and two dealership factors. Trust of the brand is the most influential factor in predicting a consumer's intent to repurchase.

value, or manufacturer's suggested retail price (MSRP) as the motivation behind our decision to choose one brand over another, but the *real* reason behind our choice—more often than not—is that owning a particular brand simply makes us *feel* better.

In the competitive automotive industry, functional aspects of the brand's product—like quality and reliability—are table stakes used to narrow down options, but they don't build strong emotional ties with consumers. When you think about a positive experience that moved you to action, you likely felt one or more of the following key motivators:

- **Trust.** You embraced the brand's premise. You accepted that its message was true, and you believed that you could trust it to deliver on its promise.

- **Confidence.** You felt that the brand had quality products and competent people to meet your needs. You perceived the brand as a leader.

- **Connection.** You trusted that the brand had integrity and compassion and would take care of you well after the new car smell had faded. You wore the brand logo because you were proud to be part of the brand community.

- **Alignment.** You saw yourself in the brand. It fit your personality and aligned with your personal values.

Not surprisingly, we found that elements of these key motivators are the primary drivers behind consumers' commitment to the dealership for servicing their vehicle *and* their intent to repurchase from the same manufacturer in the future. Moreover, these factors—along with a few others—contribute to a consumer's emotional connection to the brand in a *cumulative* way. In essence, a consumer's commitment to the brand increases relative to the number of key motivators the consumer attributes to the brand. (See Figures 12.1 and 12.2.)

What might surprise you is that feelings about the service department at the dealership shape perceptions about the brand, and vice versa. Marketers often treat sales and service as mutually exclusive, but the reality is that they're highly dependent on one another. What we'll show is that when the consumer trusts the brand *and* the dealership, it results in an amplification effect on business outcomes.

Intent to Repurchase

It's all about trust. People are more likely to repurchase from a brand they trust. Of the consumers who reported that they trust the manufacturer of their vehicle, nearly 80 percent expressed the intent to repurchase their next vehicle from the same manufacturer.

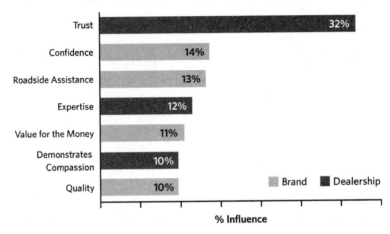

Figure 12.2 Commitment to the dealership for service is a function of three dealership factors and four brand factors. Trust of the dealership is the most influential factor.

(See Figure 12.3.) Conversely, 40 percent of low-trust respondents conveyed that they intend to repurchase from the same brand.

Without trust, functional aspects of the brand's product do little to inspire repurchase. Consider the following, shown in Figure 12.4.

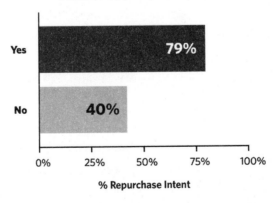

Figure 12.3 High levels of trust mean a higher likelihood of repurchasing.

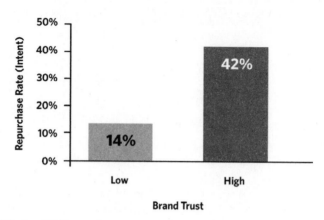

When the Brand Delivers on Quality and Value

Figure 12.4   While important, quality and value alone don't retain consumers.

We asked those consumers who indicated that they were completely satisfied with the quality and value of their vehicle whether they trusted the brand. Of those who expressed a low level of trust, only 14 percent were considering repurchasing from the same brand. The intent to repurchase jumped to 42 percent for those who expressed a high level of trust.

As the cornerstone of emotional connection, trust not only leads to customer retention, but also lays the groundwork for brand evangelism. When asked if they would recommend the manufacturer of their vehicle to a friend or family member, 93 percent of consumers with a high level of brand trust said yes. (See Figure 12.5.) In contrast, only 46 percent of consumers with a low level of brand trust reported that they would recommend the brand.

Our research found that quality and value for the money accounted for only 20 percent of a customer's intent to repurchase. The other 80 percent was explained by emotional factors representing the entire ownership experience.

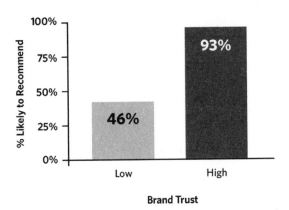

People Recommend Brands They Trust

Figure 12.5 Recommendations are driven by trust, further amplifying its impact.

The Dealership Must Deliver on the Promise

Dealerships are the retail face for vehicle brands, and the bond between consumer and service department accounts for nearly one-third of the variability of future purchase intent.

The power of dealership *brand* to influence future vehicle purchase decisions is born of the fact that consumers interact almost exclusively with dealerships and rarely (if at all) with the factory. In a real sense, consumers only know their dealership. It's the dealership that presents the vehicle, negotiates the price, and then travels with the consumer through years of ownership and driving. It's the dealership that provides service and advice in times of mechanical failure, and very likely it's the dealership that enters into a consumer's mailbox and in-box throughout the ownership experience with offers for service and tires and so much else standing as milestones on the arc of a vehicle owner's experience.

Consumers were more than twice as likely to report repurchase intent if they indicated that they trusted only the dealership to work on their vehicle. (See Figure 12.6.)

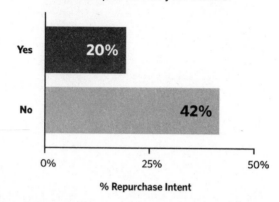

The Dealership Experience

"Would you trust anyone other than the
dealership to service your vehicle?"

Figure 12.6   The dealership experience is closely tied to a consumer's
intent to repurchase from the brand.

The Impact of Recalls

Until now, we've talked about the positive influence of factors such as
trust, integrity, and quality vis-à-vis commitment and repurchase rates.
But what happens when there's a brand recall? Is there a negative impact
that would suggest that emotion cuts both ways? The answer depends
on how the manufacturer handles the recall.

Recalls are ubiquitous across the auto industry, and while consumers may feel inconvenienced by the news of a recall, our research
suggests that recalls do little to disrupt the emotional connection a
consumer has with a brand. In fact, if the manufacturer initiates the
recall, it might actually *strengthen* the relationship.

Consider the following example from a large automotive import
manufacturer. Beginning in late 2009, the company initiated several
recalls related to a faulty accelerator pedal that ultimately impacted
over nine million vehicles. According to our survey, nearly two-thirds
of owners were aware of the recall. Yet, when we compared the repurchase intent of those who were aware of the recall versus those who

weren't, the repurchase intent was actually *higher* for those who were aware of the recall. The implication is that trust is tied to perception, and more often than not, transparency will win a brand favor with the public.

Commitment to the Dealership (Service)

Our research indicates that the dealership's service department plays a pivotal role in igniting the emotional connections that lead to brand loyalty. Consumers with a high level of commitment to the dealership were far more likely than low-commitment respondents to cite trust as a key determinant. (See Figure 12.7.)

Furthermore, when asked why they have their car serviced at the dealership, consumers with a high level of commitment to the dealership were more likely to cite factors such as community involvement and thoughtfulness than their low-commitment counterparts. While important, factors such as convenience and quality of work were less correlated with commitment level.

Positive Experiences × Meaningful Engagements = Dealership Commitment

Independently, both positive experiences (e.g., service, convenience, etc.) and meaningful engagements (e.g., following the brand on Twitter, liking the brand on Facebook, etc.) drive dealership commitment. However, when combined, the return on experience and engagement is amplified. On a scale of 1 to 10, where 10 is totally committed to the dealership, consumers with a high number of positive brand experiences and meaningful engagements scored an 8.5. By comparison, consumers with a low number of positive experiences and meaningful engagements scored only a 2.4. (See Figure 12.8.)

The implication is that the service department is instrumental in creating emotional connections with consumers that ultimately lead to

Service Extends Beyond the Vehicle

"Why do you have your car serviced at the dealership?"	High	Low	% Lift
Don't trust anyone else for this work	19%	8%	133%
Is active in the community	15%	9%	95%
Good value for the money	30%	16%	89%
Cares about people, not just profits	32%	18%	85%
Extras they give me	29%	17%	70%
They know what the service code means	44%	28%	57%
They do good work	69%	48%	45%
Convenient hours of operation	50%	35%	44%
I can pay with my preferred method of payment	26%	18%	41%
They use parts made by the company that made my vehicle	59%	43%	37%
Convenient location	50%	45%	10%

Figure 12.7 Consumers with a high level of commitment to the dealership were more likely than others to cite factors such as community involvement and compassion for people as influencers.

service *and* brand loyalty. In effect, the service department serves as an *extension* of the sales group.

The Amplification Effect in Action

In the early part of this book, we established the basic tenets of ROE²:

When positive experiences are combined with meaningful engagements, they produce an amplification effect on brand and business equity.

Now we're showing how ROE^2 can be created and measured in the real world—in this case, the automotive marketplace. We began by calculating a composite score based on a consumer's self-reported commitment to the dealership for service and intention to repurchase from the brand. We call this ROE^2 (Return on Experience × Engagement).

Next, we calculated the total number of self-reported positive experiences and meaningful engagements from an extensive list of possibilities, and classified each consumer as low, medium, or high for each dimension.

Finally, we calculated the average composite score based on commitment to the dealer for servicing and intent to repurchase from the

Dealer Commitment by Experience and Engagement Level

DEALERSHIP COMMITMENT LEVEL	Experiences		
	High	Med	Low
High	8.5	6.6	4.0
Med	7.4	5.1	3.1
Low	6.3	5.0	2.4

(Engagements axis labeled along left side)

Figure 12.8 When asked how committed they were to the dealership (on a scale of 1 to 10), consumers with the highest combination of positive experiences and meaningful engagements averaged 8.5.

brand (ranging from 1 to 50) for each combination of experience and engagement level. The resulting matrix, presented in Figure 12.9, shows the relative impact of experience and engagement on brand and business equity.

What we found is remarkable. When analyzed separately, the quality and number of experiences a consumer has with a brand are *far more* important than the quality and number of engagements. Brand and business equity increases dramatically as the number of positive experiences increase, but it is less impacted by the number of meaningful engagements. This makes sense because meaningful engagements are the *result* of emotionally charged connections stemming from positive experiences.

Proof of the Amplification Effect

BRAND & BUSINESS EQUITY—Index	Positive Experiences		
	High	Med	Low
High	128	106	85
Med	124	99	64
Low	117	81	46

Meaningful Engagements (row axis)

Figure 12.9 On their own, positive experiences increase commitment and repurchase intent. However, when positive experiences are combined with meaningful engagement, the resulting impact is amplified—delivering higher ROE².

When we evaluated them together, we found that positive experience and meaningful engagement combine to amplify the return. Emotionally charged connections are ignited by the experiences we have browsing the showroom, negotiating our trade-in, and having the vehicle serviced. Once engaged, it's our emotions that give meaning to each interaction and ultimately reinforce our perceptions—and *passion*—for the brand.

Part Three
An ROE² Primer

So far in *Igniting Customer Connections*, we've seen empirical evidence that by multiplying experience and engagement you can dramatically impact your company's bottom line. But in our increasingly complex world, the real question is this: How do you build customer connections without creating an overwhelming amount of complexity?

It sounds so simple. You need great *content* to send a relevant, compelling message to your customers, multiple digital (and traditional) *channels* to deliver that message in an effective way and at the right time, accurate *measurement* to determine the level of success in achieving your goal and to improve your approach and content, and *technology* to fuel the process in real time.

But it's complicated. Each of these four key elements poses a unique set of challenges. Each has evolved significantly during the digital disruption of advertising and marketing—and continues to change. Your organization's ability to pick the right approach and tools makes a big difference. Plus, each of the capabilities must not only enable the others, but also enhance them. This tight alignment requires close collaboration and management. What is the consequence of not getting these elements to work together? Imagine a beautiful car without an engine, or a smooth highway without a car.

I can't tell you how many times I have worked with companies that have invested millions of dollars in a data platform, only to find that they're not able to activate the data in the channels. Or companies that have beautiful, top-notch creative approaches that can't be effectively personalized in a digital world. Or (my favorite) organizations that are spending millions of dollars on marketing with virtually no effective measurement system in place.

This final part of the book takes a look at the underlying elements that fuel Return on Experience × Engagement (ROE²) and ignite new customer connections. It defines and drills down into the details of each element, highlighting trends and challenges. And it provides you with clear strategies and next steps that let you start making ROE² an integral part of your marketing efforts—no matter how small or large your organization is, what your market segment is, or the customers you serve.

Chapter 13
Content

Connecting with More Customers Starts with More (and More Relevant) Content

E very consumer is familiar with content, since consumers see lots of it every day. They may define it as advertising, information, a marketing offer, a tweet, a Facebook post, or more. But it's all content. Consumers tell us what content they value by engaging with it. And in our omnichannel world, multiple channels demand much more content—and better content. Here we take a look at the changing role of content, the growth of content marketing, and how you can put high-quality content to work to inspire customer connections.

Content and ROE^2: The Content Connection

It's simple. Compelling content is the key component of Return on Experience × Engagement (ROE^2). Content drives emotion, and emotion fuels experience—ideally, a great experience because, as the adage attributed to legendary ad man Bill Bernbach goes, *you can't bore people into buying your product*. And you definitely can't bore, cajole, intimidate, impress, or annoy them into engaging with your brand. You need to create content that gets their attention, amuses them, captivates their imagination, creates a compelling offer, and makes them want more.

Like a hit song, you know it when you hear it. And it always sounds easier and simpler to create than it is.

Experience is the key aspect of content that relates to ROE². Experience involves consumers and gets them talking, and then gets other consumers involved. And that engagement can't be forced. It has to be earned. Only honestly informative or entertaining content that garners consumer involvement will generate that emotional connection to drive experience. Bad content, boring advertising, content built from off-target strategies that don't truly engage—these will fail.

In a way, ROE² capitalizes on the equity your brand already has and the equity that it can build via more consumer involvement and connection with your brand. Experience that builds engagement also builds equity. And experience must be earned.

Content Defined

There are many, many definitions of marketing content. Some are slightly confusing, inaccurate, and overly academic. For example, an *Ad Age* article on the subject stated, "First, content resides on owned or earned media. If there's a media buy involved, it's advertising, not content marketing. Second, content marketing is a pull, rather than a push, strategy. Content doesn't interrupt, it attracts" ("What Is Content Marketing?," Rebecca Lieb, *Ad Age*, February 12, 2012).

While the rest of the description may be kind of formal, it's definitely true that *content attracts*. The degree to which it attracts consumers can be measured on what we at Epsilon call Consumer Assigned Value. Consumers tell marketers how much they value content by their level of engagement (click, watch/read, share, blog, and beyond). The rest is just advertising or marketing communication.

A brand, company, or individual brings content to a consumer, using a brand's assets to generate consumer interest, individual engagement, and cultural involvement. In short, content is the stuff that works, the stuff that gets people involved—sharing, engaging with a brand and other consumers, and feeling positively inclined toward the asset being promoted. Content is the *good stuff* that people notice, talk about, and share. Content is everything that rises above the clutter and noise online and beyond, such as:

- The ad that transcends its media buy and ends up posted all over Facebook
- The poster or print ad so good that it's art unto itself
- The tweet that everyone retweets
- The online video that touches the heart or fires the imagination
- The Super Bowl ad that plays over and over long after the game

Content is the communication that transcends its original marketing or advertising mission. Through its originality, outrageousness, quality, usefulness, or entertainment (or other intangible value), this content involves and engages people in a way that influences them—and the broader popular culture.

How Has Content Evolved?

Content isn't new, of course. It has been around in one form or another for many years. There are many examples of advertising imagery or promotional messages that transcended their original purpose and entered the popular culture—for example:

- **Collectible posters.** Original, vintage posters for many products (or films and beyond) have become highly sought-after art, since they feature timeless design and artistry that transcend the original sales messages.
- **TV and radio.** Branded content, including radio and TV programs, were longtime staples of their mediums. Content that engaged, entertained, and created cultural touchstones was brought to viewers by some of the biggest brands of the time, from Procter & Gamble on down.

- **Brand characters.** Characters that began as product spokesmen for brands have evolved into icons. Think Ronald McDonald, Toucan Sam, the Pillsbury Doughboy, the GEICO Gecko, and more.

Key Content Trends

The *good stuff*, whatever it is, has a way of being discovered—no matter what the era. But as with all other processes, the pace of the whole content continuum—from creation to connecting with consumers to sharing to end of life—has picked up considerably. Today, through the many free channels that are available, as well as paid media, compelling content can get out in the world and get shared much more quickly than ever before. (See Figure 13.1.) Or it can be ignored (or worse, ridiculed) just as fast.

Here are just some of the trends in content that marketers need to know.

Figure 13.1 Content that is truly compelling can have a life far outside its original purpose, entering the popular culture.

- **Getting the message.** The media or advertising message itself can be the content that the consumer values, and can create value for the brand that sponsors it. With various rich-media approaches, a display ad, e-mail message, or homepage takeover can be memorable, entertaining, and compelling.

- **Sharing is free—and powerful.** The ability of the consumer to pass along content *free of cost* creates whole new levels of engagement, relevance, and social connectivity.

- **Truth and transparency.** The ability to create and measure this unpaid-for exposure inspires a level of "truthiness" and transparency that didn't necessarily exist before. For example, if consumers like a specific piece of content enough, they'll pass it along and encourage the conversation to continue among other consumers. In many cases, this honest evaluation of content (and subsequent *liking/sharing* of it via social media) happens without funding from the content provider, although it can also be helped along with paid-for exposure.

- **The hunger for content.** Fast, easy distribution of content also triggers more hunger for compelling content than ever before—and a strong need to create more and more and more of it, all the time.

- **Personalization.** Consumers expect content to be customized to their interests, needs, and wants and to be placed at the right juncture in a path to purchase (now, more of a *zone*). As we will see in subsequent chapters on technology and channels, there is more data and decision making available at each point of connection—but it's all fueled by content.

- **Content is global.** When thinking about content, it's important to recognize that it may be deployed globally by the brand or by consumers. So you need to keep in mind issues of language personalization and/or translation and (even more importantly) cultural appropriateness.

- **The offer and call to action are content.** The action you are trying to motivate the consumer to take (or behavior you want the
  customer to exhibit) is part of your content strategy. It may be
  embedded in a larger piece of content or it may stand alone, but
  it's definitely content.

Content Challenges

Your organization faces many challenges when it decides to make highly
engaging, entertaining, and informative content. Here are just a few of
them:

- **Too many chefs in the kitchen.** There may be not just too many
  chefs, but too many uninformed or ill-informed chefs. Everyone
  has an opinion as to what's funny or not funny, what's entertaining or not entertaining, and what must be included or can't be
  included. And few are shy about sharing their opinions. Just watching a season of *Mad Men* seems to entitle every middle manager to
  unleash his or her inner art director. Unless the goal of the content
  is clear, the management process clear, and the approval process
  streamlined, content can become simply longer-form clutter.

- **Death by committee.** Messages and content are often crafted by
  committee think. As a result, there are many rounds of meetings
  with lots of input from many, many clients and agency personnel.
  Every "I have a concern" is addressed, and every "That scares me" is
  eliminated. Too often this approach results in bland messages that
  don't engage the consumer. If you wonder why your message isn't
  connecting and why you're not seeing results, your content creation
  process may be the problem. When you eliminate absolutely all
  risk, every edge, and every single facet of a communication that
  might elicit comment or commentary, you eliminate all hope of
  extraordinary results.

- **A high miss-to-hit ratio.** Even when you have a talented content
  team (or agency) that follows best practices, the chances of

developing breakthrough content are slim. Consider the Hollywood model of content creation. Of the many, many pilots the experts in Hollywood will look at, winnow through, and produce, the vast majority will underperform or fail outright. In fact, the ultimate failure rate will be almost 90 percent. You can expect that branded entertainment content will achieve a high failure rate, though ideally not that high. This fact means that your investment strategy must be sound and you must maximize *all* the opportunities to succeed (the right cliché here is *don't put all your eggs in one basket*)—all while not funding so stingily as to ensure failure (and here it's *being penny wise and pound foolish*).

- **Lack of experts.** Since content is evolving, it's hard to find qualified content experts or managers. Past experience in broadcast, journalism, or related media fields is relevant, but it's important to approach content marketing with a new, forward-thinking approach that recognizes its unique opportunities, while avoiding the risks we're exploring in this list.

- **Content management.** Managing the ever-growing collection of content—including personalized versions, translations, and more—raises technical challenges that need to be addressed with a robust content management solution. The specifics of this solution will vary depending on the size, focus, and pace of your organization, but content management is both a technical and a personnel challenge. You need the right technology, as well as the talented people to manage, run, and evolve it on an ongoing basis.

- **What is viral?** Viral content—largely video—is still a relatively new medium. There are still lessons being learned in terms of formats, lengths, and what works and doesn't work. Movies, radio programs, and TV shows constantly evolved in much the same way. There is still a large learning curve, and there is constant change. In short, there's no proven formula for going viral or capturing a mass audience. If there were one, all content would succeed.

- **Unclear goals.** The end result you'd like to achieve with your content must be clear from the start. Do you want exposure in the news media? A thousand *likes* on Facebook? Without a clear goal, you can't measure your success. Very often, the goal is simply to feed the content machine.

Avoid the Pitfalls of Content Creation

Too often the marketing and advertising departments of big (and small) companies avoid sending out compelling or engaging messages in favor of sending out messages that are:

1. **Overloaded.** They're chock-full of many messages, including every single reason anyone would ever want to buy the product. The consumer's eyes begin to glaze over.

2. **Too careful.** Politically sensitized messages are neutered or crafted in such a way as to absolutely, positively offend no one. The result? A message that is simply bland and ignored by everyone.

3. **Too inward-focused.** Messages that pander to the internal decision makers of a company about heritage, history, or "how the sausage is made" often violate the cardinal rule of *not boring the audience.* They aren't interesting or compelling to the customer.

Content Advice for Marketers

We've explored some of the main challenges of content. Now let's turn to overcoming those challenges. My advice for creating the content that can fuel ROE^2? Here are some key points to consider:

- **Respect the power of content.** Content can do more to put a face and a personality on your brand than any other single communication. The values of your brand can often be better expressed through content than through any other communication. Investing in breakthrough content lets you do more than feed the many hungry digital channels. It helps differentiate your organization and its products or services, engage more customers, and ultimately increase revenues.

- **Content marketing builds your brand.** Content marketing is a powerful tool that can build your brand perhaps better than any other communication. Modern data-mining capabilities give you better insights into your customers than ever before, and better ways of connecting with them one-on-one. You are in possession of a valuable secret network to reach your customers, and better insights into what will engage and entertain them. Use this tool now.

- **Know your values—and your customers.** Start by recognizing and respecting your brand's core values in every piece of content you create, from a tweet to a multitouch, omnichannel campaign with lots of moving parts. Find out what your customers are truly interested in. What do they watch, purchase, and engage with of their own free will? Look for ways to create content that will not only reflect your brand's key values but also intersect with your consumers' true interests.

- **Don't be boring.** There are lots of things that organizations shouldn't be these days (e.g., evil, uncool, or boring). Content is your opportunity to educate, engage, and charm your way into your customers' psyches and actions. Use it. And resist the tendency to stick with the status quo. Be willing to throw out the rule book and take smart, well-thought-out risks. If you expect a 10 percent return on revenue, recognize that you are going to have to take an equal risk to get there. You can't just send out a laundry list of selling points about your product to the public via every available channel—in a nonengaging or noninvolving way—and expect to clear the shelves or to be the brand that sticks in people's minds.

- **Engage with the culture.** If you want to become a major brand—one that a significant part of the population uses and thinks about on a regular basis—you need to become a part of the culture. To achieve this lofty goal, you need compelling content and a streamlined process for creating it. The rewards are clear. By engaging and entertaining the population in some meaningful way, you can grow market share.

- **Recognize the influence of time.** Time influences content, and content influences time. *When* a piece of content is deployed is a critical aspect of your strategy, since the combination of time and content creates experience. And content can build on itself through a series of atomic moments of truth.

Tap the Power of Content Marketing

Marketers should seek to evaluate their data in a new context and use their proprietary information to engage and involve their consumers to maximize their benefits. Think of yourself as the holder of vast information about what your customers like, the holder of huge virtual networks (your e-mail lists and data). Consider yourself an expert with a unique knowledge of and ability to create entertaining and engaging vehicles that will allow you to provide a great *experience* for more people (one of the all-important *E*s in ROE²) that leads your company to deeper levels of *engagement* (the other *E*), and ultimately to monetizing on that engagement.

Chapter **14**
Channels

More Paths Than Ever Lead You to Your Audience—But Reaching Them Is Just the Beginning

O n the surface, the proliferation of digital channels seems like a boon to professional marketers—more ways to reach your target audience should mean new opportunities to deliver a compelling message or offer, and to deepen the customer connection and boost sales. But there's more to channels than access. Here we take a look at the evolving channel-scape, and how to focus on improving the customer experience across all channels.

Channels Defined

Let's start with a clear definition of *channels*, as used in the context of marketing. A marketing channel is the place where the brand meets the customer. (See Figure 14.1.) It's a platform, chosen by the customer or the brand, that deploys content based on what is known about the customer and related circumstances along with associated business rules—all to enable the customer's interaction with a brand (ideally at an atomic moment of truth).

As we all know, channels have been evolving rapidly during the past dozen years or so.

*All Channels Lead
to the Consumer*

Figure 14.1   All channels lead to the consumer, and there are more channels than ever.

Historically, marketers thought of channels as broadcast, direct mail, and print, because those were the first channels we had available to us. Or there were also more human-focused channels, like branch sales, retail point of sale, and telemarketing. But the dramatic growth—the real story (and the focus of the rest of this chapter)—is in digital channels, of course. Inbound and outbound, online, direct, social, mobile, web, e-commerce—these digital channels are completely changing how marketers reach consumers, and vice versa.

Take a Closer Look at Digital Channels

You can divide digital channels into a few different categories— acquisition channels, direct channels, and social channels.

- **Acquisition channels.** These channels drive new (primarily anonymous) interactions between brands and consumers. For example, search engine marketing (SEM), search engine optimization (SEO), and site-based online advertising are all examples of channels that enable brands to acquire new customers. These channels are powerful, but because they are largely anonymous it can be hard to apply Return on Experience × Engagement (ROE^2). This is starting to change, as we can now begin to target unique audiences through targeted display and targeted social interactions.

- **Direct channels.** These channels support and/or drive ongoing engagement and interactions with known (or partially known) individuals, directly. For example, website (on-site) content, information, and support; audience-based online targeting and retargeting; e-mail and short message service (SMS); location-based messaging; and loyalty programs are all different direct channels.

- **Social channels.** These channels—including front-runners like Facebook and Twitter, plus socially driven information sites like Yelp or travel-focused review sites—have created platforms for brand engagement that are driven more by consumer interactions *with each other*, not just with the keepers of the brand. Among the marketing activities here you'll find social media targeted advertising, engagement tools (sweeps and games), informational engagement (calculators and tools), and user-generated content such as customer opinion (likes and reviews) and blogs and point-of-view (POV) posts.

In general, the common theme of these channels (with the exception of pure acquisition channels) is that they offer increasingly sophisticated ways of identifying consumers or profiles, managing and deploying content for customers, and collecting more and more detailed data about the interaction.

What Does Cross-Channel Marketing Mean to the Consumer? And to You?

The other theme of today's channels arises from their expansion and proliferation. Now that there are multiple channels, cross-channel marketing recognizes that consumers use multiple channels leading up to a well-informed purchase. And that cross-channel may mean different things to various consumers. For example, a purchase cycle, or arriving at a purchasing zone, might involve the following channel-based interactions:

- Exposure (frequent) to advertising on the web, radio, or TV
- Active product research on the web
- Reviews on social media
- Referrals from social media
- Phone or in-person interaction driven by the customer or brand
- Interaction through brand websites and e-mails, driving engagement and leading to the desired interactions, often involving a series of steps from initial inquiry through purchase, activation, and use.

Coordinating, timing, and ensuring consistency across all these channels (touch points, if you will) are major challenges faced by today's marketers.

Interactions Create the Consumer Experience

Another way to think about the cumulative effect of all these channel interactions is through the lens of ROE². This collection of cross-channel interactions delivers the experiences that define the brand for a consumer—and that lead to a purchase decision and form customer engagement. In the past, this customer experience was more easily controlled, since there were fewer interactions, because marketers retained control, and because the overall path to a purchase decision was more linear.

Not anymore. The customer experience—and the expectation of what that experience will entail—has shifted and metamorphosed along with the rest of the world of marketing.

How Have Customer Expectations Changed?

Consumers (and ultimately, customers) want to be informed. They want to be in control. And they take control by collecting and sharing information online and socially. They have choices and they investigate them. These developments and more reduce their overall loyalty and barrier to change such as switching brands. And customers expect that the context (look and feel, messaging, history with the brand) will carry through every interaction.

What else has changed? Purchase decisions are more cautious, as consumers take control of the process, do more research, and take full advantage of all of the many sources of information and advice available to them. After all, thanks to our information-rich, Internet-driven world, there's an ever-expanding amount of widely available information (first- and third-party) about products and more. And experiences, particularly fantastic or terrible, can be shared socially and made available to the world. As a result, brand loyalty is minimal and fleeting in this era of shorter attention spans. And brands need to work much harder to garner loyalty. Customers are loyal to an *experience*, one that is sensitive to the value of their time and their need for information, and that shows the ongoing commitment of the brand.

What Makes a Great or Terrible Customer Experience?

Customer experiences are wildly subjective, of course, based on individual tastes and expectations. But here are some examples:

- **A great customer experience** is consistent throughout all the channels that customers choose, delivering the information they need, when they need it—all in a timely fashion, and all reflecting the cumulative experience of the customer. It delights the customer by sending an incredibly compelling message (and ultimately, an offer) that is based on the customer's needs and that meets or exceeds those needs. It delivers value and makes the customer feel good about taking the next step. And after the experience is over, the customer feels so pleased by the experience and the end result that he or she shares it with the world. (See Figure 14.2.)

- **A bad customer experience** is tone-deaf to the needs of customers and fails to give them the information they need, in the way that they need it. Other characteristics? Too much or too little contact. Bad timing. The wrong level of detail. The wrong channel. And lack of compelling content. Think of a badgering used car salesperson, refusing to listen to your needs and simply bothering you on the phone and via e-mail (or as an example of bad use of channels, via your circa-1995 fax machine) with offers on cars you can't imagine

What Makes a
Great Experience?

Figure 14.2   The definition of a great experience varies, which makes it all the more important to know what your diverse consumers want and need. But everyone knows that a bad experience feels like.

ever driving. That's what a bad customer experience feels like, and we've all had plenty of them, in the physical world and online.

Key Channel Trends

Here are five major trends to know about when you think about how to best combine, configure, and cadence channels in your own marketing, no matter how small or large your organization:

1. As media proliferate, the search for effective brand exposure complicates.
2. New customer experience models are disrupting and redefining commerce.
3. Mobile is no longer a channel; it's a platform.
4. Consumers are in control, and their expectations are high.
5. Social media is a beast.

As Media Proliferate, the Search for Effective Brand Exposure Complicates

The average consumer's exposure to message-bearing media has increased from less than 20 percent of the day 40 years ago to more than 100 percent of the day, due to access to multiple channels simultaneously and consistently throughout the day via television, radio, and Internet-based media accessed via desktop, mobile device, and beyond.

The implications? The growing number of channels can be used to target different customer segments at different stages of their journeys and life cycles. And there is tremendous and ever-increasing competition for customer attention, thanks to the proliferation (and low cost) of these media-driven channels. In short, every brand is fighting for attention, and simply shouting louder won't necessarily get that attention.

New Customer Experience Models Are Disrupting and Redefining Commerce

Customer experiences, once grounded in the real world, are now embedded in digital channels as digitally oriented consumers veer further into the mobile and social aspects of their world. These experiences are being developed in every industry, disrupting legacy business models. Why? Because customers find these experiences more useful, efficient, enjoyable, and informative, as well as easier to share.

Examples? In the media world, ESPN is using social gaming (fantasy sports, prediction-based games, and beyond) to drive interaction with online and televised sports news and live broadcasts. And in transportation, the next-generation car service, Uber, uses a mobile application to drive access to (and increased demand for) a luxury experience—in effect, a black-car taxi service—all while opening up a new market for black car service providers, since Uber's model is built on the short-haul, no-reservation needs of today's customer. And in retail, Amazon is driving participation in its Amazon Prime service by providing a compelling combination of expedited shipping, the ability to *borrow* e-books, and other premium experiences.

What do these examples show? That companies that want to thrive need to rethink their business models to ensure that digital channels are at the core of their marketing, not just added on. Creating great customer experiences via the right combination of channels is the key to triggering the desired result.

Mobile Is No Longer a Channel; It's a Platform

Mobile treatment is something that must be considered in all dimensions of your strategy. The proliferation and popularity of mobile smartphones, tablets, and other mobile devices, coupled with the availability of multiple channels on each device (search, web, social, e-mail, proprietary apps, location-based apps), all put mobile ahead of the desktop as the primary access to digital channels. In short, mobile has emerged as a platform that will drive access to customers via various social and digital channels. And as the platform of choice, the content format, messaging type (e-mail, SMS, in-app, native, etc.), location awareness, and mobile/social applications must all be adapted to the various devices that are available.

For you, as a marketer, the shifting popularity of devices means staying in touch with (and ensuring awareness of) how consumers are using devices and capabilities at any point in time, such as:

- Turning on their iPads or tablets and checking e-mail when they wake up
- Using their smartphones during their commute or while traveling
- Relying on their desktop computers while working
- Using their smartphones and location-based apps when shopping or dining
- Turning to their iPads again when they're back at home in front of the TV

Consumers Are in Control, and Their Expectations Are High

Each customer's specific preferences will determine a buying process customized to that customer—including the channels and platforms (devices used), as well as where information is sourced, the length of the buying cycle, the attributes of the products that person will buy, and the price he or she is willing to pay. In the past, brands were the main source of information about their products, benefits, and customer experiences. But with the proliferation of information coming from sources other than the brand—including social media and new channels and devices—brands can expect a more demanding customer with ever-escalating expectations in terms of the quality and level of personalization of each interaction.

What does this all mean? Now the customer chooses the timing and channel of interaction. The customer expects awareness of recent interactions, regardless of channel. And customers expect a brand to be aware of their preferences—and comply with them across all interactions. In short, customers expect a lot. And these expectations keep growing.

Social Media Is a Beast

As an evolving element only partially in the control of marketers, social media presents many challenges, as any marketer knows. Simply being part of the latest social media platform isn't enough. The challenge is to harness the positive power of social media (viral content, consumer-created content, and much more) while avoiding its downside (trolls, competitors masquerading as citizens, etc.). The trend toward integration of social media into marketing continues, of course. But it's balanced by a need to see measurable, attributable results.

Channel Challenges for Marketers

Trying to deliver a great cross-channel customer experience? Here are five challenges that can make it difficult:

1. Fast change—keeping pace with dramatic change
2. Big Data—making sense of massive volumes of data
3. Customer recognition—identifying customers across all channels
4. Real-time cross-channel interaction—delivering a high-quality experience
5. Complex measurement—measuring cross-channel interaction

Fast Change—Keeping Pace with Dramatic Change

New marketing/media channels are emerging quickly and regularly, and consumers are adopting them just as quickly. Staying on top of this evolution is a challenge. For example, we have seen a significant evolution of friend-to-friend messaging during the past decade, as customer preference moved along this progression:

E-mail > Facebook > Twitter > Snapchat

This change dramatically alters the mechanisms required for marketers to understand sentiment, identify opportunities, and reach consumers directly. After all, to interact with consumers means staying in touch with where they prefer to be online, versus being marginalized. The variety of interactions across channels that include inbound, outbound, offline, online, real-time, and more keeps complexity high and makes delivering personalized content difficult, as does the likelihood that consumer interactions will take place via third-party, social, or web channels.

What can organizations do to keep pace? Since it's expensive to continuously improve and expand solutions and infrastructure, it's important to focus on key strategic interactions (commerce, content creation, customer experience). Leverage services to gain access to emerging channels, help manage data, and analyze processes—as well as for targeting, media, and ongoing marketing interactions. In short, focus your infrastructure where it matters, and rely on well-selected services elsewhere.

Big Data—Making Sense of Massive Volumes of Data

The proliferation of media and social interactions across many channels is creating a high volume of data. Ever-expanding data isn't news anymore. But storage, organization, analysis, and use of huge volumes of rapidly growing structured and unstructured data remain serious challenges for any organization.

In the past, restrictions on data access, storage, and analysis limited centralization of data to campaign-level metadata, the history of direct promotions (direct mail, e-mail, phone), and purchase history. Interaction data from the web was generally limited to local analysis to drive site efficiency and to understand use from a media point of view.

Now the boundaries have crumbled thanks to better, faster, and cheaper technology. Growing demand from marketers who want to store and analyze data has driven the Big Data industry to realize that marketing is a primary application. The types of data that are stored and analyzed now include those listed in Figure 14.3.

Marketers want to be able to gather and store structured and unstructured data to support analyses of customers, channels, offers, interaction, and specific content. And these capabilities are evolving to become more readily available, simpler to use, and less expensive. We explore Big Data in more detail in Chapter 17.

An Overview of Consumer Data	
Customer identifier by channel	Surveys and opinions
Customer context at time of interaction	Phone interaction data (voice, etc.)
Interaction record and detail (local)	Cookie-based web interaction data
History of promotional data	Mobile activity
Content detail (with personalization)	Social media history
Business rules utilized	Click-through data
Response affected (change in context)	Social reviews and comments
Purchase history	

Figure 14.3 Thanks to more and more data about consumers, we can learn more about them than ever before.

Customer Recognition—Identifying Customers across All Channels

In the past, marketers could identify customers and link their channel-based interactions to an identity only when working with the most direct channels. This limitation lowered the ability to measure and improve effectiveness in more anonymous channels. The need to provide a more seamless brand experience for all customers is driving the need to understand the identity of these customers, as well as their online profiles. For marketers, this understanding also helps target channels more effectively, and drive a more measurable (and better) return on all marketing investments—whether SEO, SEM, social, or on third-party sites.

The implication? With more accurate customer recognition, targeting can be increasingly precise and marketers no longer have to rely on simple segmentations. For example, it's possible to match historical direct customer behavior to online behavior—dramatically improving the understanding of customers and the quality of brand experience they receive. To recognize customers across channels, marketers can rely on browser-based cookies, mobile device identifiers, and capture of interaction data for analysis. But delving into these areas requires that marketers have a high degree of comfort with current and emerging technologies—or an adept technology partner.

Real-Time Cross-Channel Interaction—Delivering a High-Quality Experience

Customer expectations for interactions are higher than ever. For marketers, the challenge is to meet these higher expectations while dealing with a much more complicated marketing landscape—one where channels have proliferated, media are being consumed at a record rate, and interactions have diversified. Consider the complexity of ensuring a high-quality experience across first- and third-party channels that can be social or mobile enabled, inbound or outbound, and offline or online. Now factor in the expectation of real-time speed, meaning that brands have to deliver a great experience *now*.

The implication for marketers is that the process of targeting, decision making, rendering content across channels, collecting interaction data, measuring results, and retargeting/decision making must happen in seconds, and must use multiple channels, either sequentially or simultaneously. After all, consumers might be on the phone while doing product research on a website, or on Facebook asking for information from friends while interacting with an online catalog.

However, remember that *real time is not always the right time*. It's important to collect and make decisions on data in real time, but the right time to deliver a message may be different. For example, if I'm watching (and tweeting, of course) about my favorite sporting event on my iPad, a brand would want to wait until the event is over before its next proactive communication.

Complex Measurement—Measuring Cross-Channel Interaction

Legacy measurement strategies for marketing attempt to correlate media investment (campaigns) with its impact on business via relatively simple and straightforward metrics—including views, clicks, visitors, and the like. These strategies provide a measurement and understanding of media effectiveness at a fairly general level. Direct marketers have slightly more sophisticated ways of viewing the impact of direct interactions on customer behavior leading to a purchase—attribution. Once a marketer acknowledges the quantity and complexity of media exposure and interactions that lead to a purchase (or another desired level of engagement), then it's clear that simpler measurement techniques—which work fairly well when modeling large numbers—become much more effective.

What does this high level of complexity mean for marketers? It highlights how important it is for all marketers—at all levels and in all industries—to develop and use new methods to understand the effectiveness of marketing investments—even if it means leaving traditional measurements behind. These emerging approaches, such as ROE^2, will use larger volumes of data, more sophisticated customer interaction definitions, and new analytic techniques.

Strategies for Improving Customer Experiences across Channels

Now that we know the trends and challenges, here are five channel strategies that you can put to work for your organization:

1. Focus on the quality of the customer experience across channels.
2. The emerging Internet of Things will create even more channels.
3. Try to understand customer interaction pathways across channels.
4. Use customer data to improve online targeting.
5. Generalize each dimension of the customer experience.

Focus on the Quality of the Customer Experience across Channels

Your brand doesn't have single-channel customers anymore. Disregard any organizational or technological boundaries that keep you from using all channels possible to improve the customer experience. Assess customer needs and expectations, and focus your efforts on meeting and exceeding them. After all, if there is an opportunity to create a better customer experience that drives a different (and more customer-oriented) business model, you need to take advantage of it. Otherwise, your competitors will. When looking at the customer experience across all channels, also consider how to achieve broader cross-channel objectives. Introduce channels with a lower understanding of customer identity and context. Tap third-party data. And consider the implications of real-time interaction across all channels—and how to make it happen.

The Emerging Internet of Things Will Create Even More Channels

The FitBit Flex fitness band, Pebble Watch, Google Glass, and iBeacons, as well as devices like automatic vehicle tracking systems, the Whistle dog tracker, and the Nest learning thermostat, are all a part of what many are describing as the "Internet of Things." These devices will track more and more information about what we personally are doing and when and where it's happening. While tied directly into the conversation about privacy, many consumers will opt in to using all of these devices as proactive channels of communication, opening new and expanded ways to influence experience and engagement.

Try to Understand Customer Interaction Pathways across Channels

Knowing how your customers interact with your brand across all channels will give you a clearer picture of the overriding (and evolving) behavioral pathways that your customers are creating. Test and measure these pathways, and use this information to improve the quality of your interactions.

Use Customer Data to Improve Online Targeting

First-party data is key to improving your online targeting. Use it to create look-alike targeting for social and online media. Look-alike models basically take a cohort of data that exhibits the sort of behavior that you want (clicking on an ad, in this case) and use the information you know about them to analyze another population to find people who look like the clickers. This can be done via advanced analytics or, for example, by looking intuitively at an audience of ski enthusiasts who click on outdoor experience ads and finding more people who look like them (under 40, interested in the environment, etc.). Personalize interactions across your websites, and retarget customers who have shown interest in your brand or interest in a specific product or service.

Generalize Each Dimension of the Customer Experience

When expanding across channels, you need to evaluate the customer experience in a channel-neutral, high-level context that considers the following general criteria:

- Customer identifier (or not)
- Customer history or context (pathway)
- Content (multiple pieces with rules for assembly)
- Business, decision, and recommendation rules
- Offers
- Response

Recognize that timing of the path to purchase can vary dramatically. These paths can be highly personalized based on specific behaviors, personalized content, and different sequences between paths. And also recognize that measurement is a challenge—from weighting the incremental impact of each exposure to addressing the complexity of attribution.

Channels Are Ever-Evolving—Just Like Your Work to Master and Maximize Them

We've covered the trends, challenges, and strategies that can help you address the critical element in reaching your customers and ensuring an excellent customer experience. But when concluding any discussion of channels, it's vital to point out that today's mix of channels—the most popular channels and the assisting channels—are always in flux based on largely uncontrollable evolution in technology advances and consumer preferences. So tomorrow's channel mix won't look like today's. Final advice? Watch how customers are using channels, and ensure that your brand is in sync, creating great customer experiences that cross all channels and taking full advantage of the specific strengths of each.

Chapter 15
Measurement and Segmentation

Segment Your Customers and Measure Your Results, Accurately and Consistently

I n many traditional marketing approaches, measurement and segmentation are two separate topics. I believe that that is a legacy of the past, when segmentation was based on limited data and was very static, and when measurement was done only on a campaign-by-campaign basis, with the results often lagging the campaign by weeks and months.

Both of these practices are central to Return on Experience × Engagement (ROE^2), but they need to be looked at in a different light and considered together. Measurement and segmentation in ROE^2 are directly connected. As we measure the impact of our marketing efforts and spend, we should be automatically feeding those learnings into whom we market to next, and how we market to them. As we saw in Part Two, many of the key drivers of business outcomes correlate not to simple demographic or transactional attributes as in the past. They come from the emotional and experience side of the equation. We need to expand the aperture of what data we are capturing and leverage this data in both measurement and segmentation.

ROE^2 is all about an objective measure that can guide a brand to determine how much to invest in driving experience and/or engagement with the customer. Here we delve into the details of measurement and segmentation and provide strategies for making them an integrated part of all your marketing, not an afterthought.

A Renewed Focus on Measurable Results

I used to hear the saying *I know that half of my marketing is effective, but I just don't know which half.* This line or its many variations, which used to get an insider-y laugh from marketers, is cringe-making now—because there isn't a company in the world that's going to tolerate that level of confusion about what's working and what's not. Maybe that's why marketing spend is relatively flat and CFOs are increasingly involved in marketing decisions—and why the average chief marketing officer (CMO) lasts just over a year in that role.

If economics is the *dismal science* (as defined by Thomas Carlyle), traditional marketing was the *opaque art*, an area of vague generalities. Not anymore. Given the wealth of consumer data available, marketers are becoming data-driven researchers, searching for insights in the mountains of data—and finding them, with varying degrees of success. Using these insights well can increase the effectiveness of campaigns significantly, and take some of the mystery out of why marketing succeeds.

Types of Measurement: An Overview

There are so many metrics out there that it's important to understand that each metric has its place. Put campaign metrics in the hands of every campaign operator, roll up channel metrics to prioritize investments, and use overall lifetime value metrics as your dependent variable. Further, go the extra mile to see how emotional factors (customer advocacy, ratings, reviews) vary with campaign and channel metrics to compile a holistic view of ROE^2.

Let's start from the bottom and work our way up:

- **Individual campaign metrics.** These metrics include clicks, conversions, downloads, responses, store transactions, phone orders, likes, forwards, content exposure, and sales. These are all important success metrics to determine how well a campaign works to meet its business objectives. They typically follow a customer life-cycle approach, from awareness to purchase consideration to purchase transaction, repeat transactions, and (eventually) brand loyalty. These measures often include things like brand awareness or familiarity (often survey-based), e-mail clicks and opens, e-commerce transactions, phone orders, and in-store purchases. Each has its place in measuring the effectiveness of campaign targeting, content design, offer motivation, frequency, and cadence.

- **Channel metrics.** Marketers often seek to understand how a channel overall is driving desired outcomes. They might look at, for example, what percentages of in-app offers drive purchases on mobile devices. Or we can see how many in-store promotions drive redemption at point of sale. For e-mail, we look at the *health* of an e-mail list as measured by longitudinal engagement over time, or length of time from sign-up to first click to understand if the value proposition for our e-mail communications resonates with customers. In display and search, response data is available with instant results on

(continued)

how well an ad or keyword is performing, and offers and
targeting can be optimized in real time through ad networks
and bidding systems. The point is that each channel has a
set of optimization metrics that can be monitored to be sure
our message is reaching the right audience at the right time
on the right device.

- **Lifetime value.** This common metric lets us understand the
value of a customer over his or her lifetime relationship with
a brand. It allows us to answer key questions such as *how
much would I spend to get a particular customer?* and *what
is the real cost of losing a customer?* It leads us in the right
direction, because we are moving beyond a traditional point
in time return on investment (ROI) of a customer metric.
But it falls short because it does not fully consider experience
and engagement to predict outcomes.

- **ROE².** As we have discussed throughout this book, ROE²
goes beyond lifetime value, as it looks at all elements of
engagement, not just buying activity, and links in the emotional or experiential connection to a brand. Lifetime value
could still be the dependent variable you are trying to drive.
But with ROE² you will get a much richer approach to predicting your business outcomes.

As marketers, we are often stuffed with data and starved for
insights. Finding insights requires understanding all of the measures
and research just discussed, and applying them to a true customer need.
It means keeping your finger on the pulse of the consumer to uncover
unseen trends, and using primary research, real-time product feedback,
reviews, and other social media input to provide actionable insights.

Because measurement in itself isn't helpful. It's what you do with what you learn that really matters.

Important Elements We're Trying to Understand

Measurement and the downstream uses of segmentation are based on incrementally and causality, two important concepts that run across all elements of measurement, and that will feed into your segmentation strategy.

1. **Incrementality** looks at the question *are we creating business outcomes that we would be getting anyway?* If a customer comes into your café every day to buy a cup of coffee and you are spending dollars advertising that coffee or incentivizing that behavior in some way, you are just cannibalizing dollars that you would already be achieving. We need to determine if a dollar is really a *new* dollar.

2. **Causality** looks at which individual marketing effort (or collection of marketing efforts) is actually causing a consumer to deliver a business outcome. This knowledge is increasingly important in an omnichannel world where so many touches are possible.

Both of these factors require careful attention when designing testing and measurement strategies. Later in this chapter we will explore the emerging science of *multichannel attribution* as a solution to these needs.

It's Really about Marketing Investment Allocation

One of the ways I often start a strategy conversation with a client is to ask what the marketing investment allocation approach is. This question is often met with a puzzled stare. Many marketers don't really think about their budgets this way. But the investment allocation is essential to implementing ROE^2 and driving business outcomes. I have yet to meet the CMO or marketing manager who has an unlimited budget. It's essential that the dollars you have are allocated to the strategies, communications, and customers that can drive the best business outcomes. (See Figure 15.1.)

For example, many organizations spend a great deal of energy marketing to their very best customers. While you certainly want to reward those customers (e.g., via loyalty programs) you also want to allocate dollars to customers who could be high-value customers in the future.

Central to your investment allocation should be the concept of potential value, not just the value you're getting from a customer today. In Part Two we saw the power of experience and engagement in increasing the share of wallet (SOW); these are the customers from whom you

Investment Allocation

	Low Potential Value	High Potential Value
High Current Value	**LOWER MARKETING INVESTMENT.** Focus on maintaining the experience with your brand.	**HIGHEST INVESTMENT.** Invest in the experience of customers who give you a lot of value today. And much more in the future.
Low Current Value	**LOWEST INVESTMENT.** Money spent in this quadrant should be reallocated.	**TARGETED INVESTMENT.** Focus on customers with high engagement or experience attributes, but who have not converted to value.

Potential Value

Figure 15.1 Knowing potential value helps you allocate your marketing investments accordingly.

are capturing most of the potential. So as we think about allocating your marketing investment dollars, how do we capture those customers with large potential—and then increase the elements of experience and engagement to optimize their performance?

The Changing Landscape of Measurement and Segmentation

The shift to using experience and engagement as factors to measure and segment by is difficult for those of us who grew up in a campaign-centric world driven by a transactional data warehouse. It's easy to look at campaign results and see how well an offer boosted awareness, inspired a purchase, or drove new registrations (whatever the case may be). What's harder—but arguably more important—is to understand the long-term impact on brand and business equity.

That's not to say transactional metrics are not important. They definitely have their place within optimizing channels and individual interactions. Better timing, more accurate targeting, and more compelling content will all help boost campaign metrics for the better—their importance stays the same. What's different is linking those actions to an overall customer journey, and measuring how well we have led more high-value customers through their next step with us. As we have seen, we can't just base our segmentation and measurement on the demographics or purchase behavior. We must include the elements of experience and the broader set of engagement attributes. Measuring these qualities is often survey-based or captured in social sentiment. But they pick up where transactional measures leave off—spotting the connection between individual interactions and lifelong loyalty.

Above all, you'll find that *ROE^2 drives long-term value.* As you broaden your view of the data that you are capturing by segmenting and measuring, use it to allocate your marketing investment to the places where it will perform best and continually evolve and adapt over time. Then you will get the business outcomes you desire.

Emotional Segmentation Emerges

Segmentation has been around since the Industrial Revolution and has been aggressively refined over the past 30 years with the advent of powerful data capture and computing capabilities. The leading practices have evolved from recency, frequency, and monetary (RFM) value to demographic, to attitudinal, and to behavioral. But I believe we are on the edge of a new form of segmentation—emotional segmentation.

As we have seen throughout the course of the book, there are powerful connections between how people *feel* about a brand and the impact on business outcomes. Couple this fact with the broad-based ability to capture data on how a customer feels through social networking and other sources, and we can now begin to segment and predict those feelings. For example:

- We can combine information about the value of a customer with his or her emotions to understand which customer should be allocated marketing dollars.

- We can use advanced analytics (machine learning) to work through the data and predict who are *about to* become emotionally involved (or uninvolved) so we can target them proactively and move them into a high state of emotional commitment.

- We can take our customers who are highly engaged and emotionally involved and build a look-alike model to find other customers or prospects we can target.

- We can segment based on emotional data items and deliver custom content to consumers that will connect with them in an extremely powerful way.

I am confident that these approaches to emotional segmentation will take off over the next couple of years—creating a segmentation revolution.

Five Trends in Measurement

Here we explore how key trends are affecting how organizations measure the impact of their marketing initiatives.

1. Start with the End

For years, marketing process charts have looked roughly the same, as shown in Figure 15.2. But as you see in the new version, I think there's another way to look at the marketing process.

The new marketing process doesn't save measurement for last.

This may sound like semantics, but when we consider the impact of ROE^2 it's critically important to start at the end and to use learnings from our measurement to determine where to look for insights—and

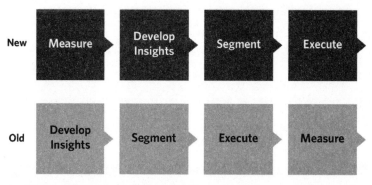

The Marketing Process

New: Measure → Develop Insights → Segment → Execute

Old: Develop Insights → Segment → Execute → Measure

Figure 15.2 The new marketing process doesn't save measurement for last.

how to segment customers into audiences. Now we can empirically measure the impact of an emotionally connected customer on a positive business outcome and understand the specific tactics that will create that connection. So this information must be the basis for developing further insights and new segments.

Further, shift your insights work from broad-based research on the category or customer, but really dive into understanding why a certain outcome happened. Do research to uncover why customers feel connected to a social community, or how a piece of content creates an emotional connection. Then use those findings to refine your segmentation, content, and communication strategies going forward. Final point—do not relegate measurement to an afterthought.

2. Data Explosion

We have touched on it multiple times in this book, but in today's digital world we are generating and managing enormous amounts and types of information. We've outlined many of the types of information you will want available to segment and measure from an ROE^2 approach. Clearly, the new digital and particularly social landscape provides a whole new world to capture data about engagement and experience. Here are some key points from a measurement and segmentation perspective:

- **Historical trend information is critical.** Be able to look back and see what a customer's disposition was around ROE^2 historically. Changes in engagement and experience are powerful predictors and key triggers for an atomic moment of truth.

- **Make sure the data is actionable.** It does you little good to draw a brilliant insight if you cannot put it into action as part of your marketing program.

- **Be flexible.** The only thing we can say for sure is that there will be a new channel, social media platform, or other way to connect to your customers over the next few years. Each of these will represent a new option to capture data that could influence your business.

3. Understand Share of Wallet

We have seen that the concept of share of wallet (SOW) is a key outcome of focusing on experience and engagement, and have discussed it in the approach to allocating your marketing investment. One question I often get asked is: How do you figure out how much your customers are spending with your competitors? Basically, there are few perfect solutions, but there are three solid approaches:

1. **Ask them via a survey.** You will be surprised to see how much your customers will tell you about their behaviors when you ask. With a survey, you can get this information from a sample of your clients and then build a model using commonly available data to extrapolate across your entire customer base.

2. **Tap third-party data.** Depending on your category, there may be a data source that compiles information across companies at the customer level. At Epsilon we have a product called Abacus that is a cooperative of more than 1,500 retailers, catalogers, nonprofits, and media companies. We also partner with a third-party company that compiles credit card spend data, which enables determination of wallet share. And there are many others.

3. **Use best demonstrated practices.** Look at the top decile of spend for a product or category. It's likely that you are capturing the majority of the spend for these customers. Then compare the rest of your customer base (possibly segmented by demographics around income, wealth, and/or geography) to size the wallet opportunity with other customers.

4. Get the Data to the People

CEOs are managing their businesses more quantitatively than ever before. Now that we have the ability to measure so many *things*, organizations need to pick a handful of metrics that truly drive the company, and must do so with transparency. This trend is true for CMOs as well. You will certainly want to measure the business outcomes that are generated by ROE^2, but once you understand the key drivers of experience and engagement for your business, you must measure and distribute that information to the whole company—whether that's just you, the marketing team, or 100,000 employees around the world.

For example, Zynga's reach, engagement, monetary metrics pervade the entire company culture. Employees are measured on how well their activities support these three key metrics for the firm. And Recyclebank—a pioneering start-up in the clean-tech Internet space—makes money by installing its program in communities and diverting waste to the recycling bin. It then rewards communities with loyalty points. Rather than focusing on moving trash, the entire enterprise is focused on Recyclebank member engagement, which educates and motivates hundreds of local communities to buy more eco-friendly products, change energy consumption patterns, and shop locally for goods and services. That's real power that extends well beyond the trash can. And it's a great example of unconventional measurement.

5. Real-Time Adaptation

It's no longer okay to have the results of a marketing effort lag days or weeks behind. In today's world, where experience and engagement can change in a second, we must be constantly measuring and adapting our strategies. The biggest changes come from the advent and proliferation of new social media tools, which put the power of shaping your brand into the hands of your customers. Social media has given us real-time access to feedback and sentiment in the marketplace. Use it first and foremost.

For example, Gap changed its logo, but then changed it back based on instant social feedback that said customers liked the old logo.

In other creative, responsive social initiatives, Hilton has been actively tweeting to people seeking restaurant recommendations in certain cities. This initiative goes beyond measurement and into involvement. But by understanding where high-value customers are spending time, Hilton is engaging with prospective customers from its @hilton handle—so it will be top of mind next time someone travels.

Five Measurement Strategies

These strategies can help your organization adjust and enhance how it measures the ultimate impact of its marketing initiatives.

1. Let Your Vision Drive Your Metrics

If you want to truly connect with consumers, you need to make sure your metrics align with your vision. For example, consider TXU Energy and its "We want you to buy less of what we make" campaign/initiative. If TXU just wanted to expand its footprint and drive more electricity consumption, it would have missed the emotional connection to the environmental movement. Instead, it measures success on consumers' involvement with energy consumption tools and education on making their households efficient. Tapping into the power of social responsibility has been rewarded handsomely with long-term loyal customers who feel they can now identify with the brand.

2. It's Not Just about the Results, but Also the Process

As you think about how you segment and measure, it's important to focus on the process your company uses to create communications. This advice holds true regardless of whether you are focusing on ROE^2, but here are a couple of important concepts to maximize your effectiveness:

- **Consistency is key.** The key to thinking about allocating your marketing dollars in the most powerful way is to measure and analyze consistent metrics across campaigns, customers, and communications. Otherwise the results won't be comparable.

- **Choose your measures of business outcomes and stick with them.** In Part Two, we saw how the various elements of experience and engagement drive amplified business outcomes. The business outcomes you choose to measure will change based on your objectives, the information you have, the size of your business, and the category of business you are in. But it's important to stick with the same metrics you are using.

3. Test, Test, Test—and Adapt

The notion of testing is central to optimizing any market strategy or campaign. It's even more important with ROE² in a digital world, because the amount of data and content is vast and the inferences as to what will drive business outcomes are endless. There are many different approaches to testing ranging from simple A/B tests for content to very sophisticated fractional (or multivariate) testing strategies that measure the impact of individual elements of content, as well as the interaction effects of those elements.

The key is to have a disciplined strategy that includes continuous testing of all marketing mix components, including new channels, content, offers segmentation, and experiences against a control. Within an ROE² framework, you will want to test how different types and levels of content can create that emotional connection, or if a different level of service will change the way someone experiences a brand.

Additionally, the ability to adapt quickly is key. For example, at Epsilon, our digital messaging platform Harmony lets you choose a desired element of engagement (opens, clicks, likes, conversions), and set up a collection of content to test; the system will automatically flip to the top-performing content after the first 10 percent of customers have been contacted.

4. Take the Longitudinal View of Performance

It's important to avoid the shortsighted trap of a campaign-focused mentality. Staying in the campaign-centric world creates a myopic view of success. Consider, for example, almost any e-commerce retailer during the holiday season. They often blast out daily e-mails announcing their latest deal or shout at you to buy now—sometimes more than once a day. Results may look favorable with any incremental dollar for that day, but in the process they are burning out their list. From an ROE^2 perspective, brands should always take a more holistic view of campaign activity, which in this case would include tracking opt-out rates and spam complaints, key measures of (dis)engagement for an e-mail program. Taken together in a long-term customer view, they would see how daily sales pushes might actually be hollowing out the brand and destroying business and brand equity.

5. Investigate Multichannel Attribution

The current state of measurement is generally *last click*. This approach basically attributes all of the value of an action (sale, conversion, registration) to the most recent communication. For example, if a customer was exposed to a TV ad, direct mail, and a display ad and then received an e-mail and clicked and purchased, 100 percent of the value of that purchase would be attributed to the e-mail. This approach would likely make e-mail look like a high-performing channel, but clearly other communications may have made an impact as well. In short, attribution is not as simple as last-click measurement, which ignores the confluence of multiple channels influencing a behavior in our interconnected, always-on world. And it's important to realize that there's a remarkable amount of back-and-forth between the web and offline sales. (See Figure 15.3.)

A new generation of solutions now entering the market uses statistical measures to determine which communications in a series of communications had an impact—and then will allocate a percentage of the value to each communication. For more sophisticated companies, custom attribution models can be created that recognize the depth and complexity of your data and customer interactions.

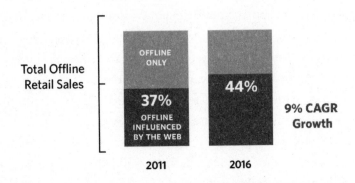

FORECAST: U.S. CROSS-CHANNEL RETAIL 2011–2016

Figure 15.3   The connection between online and traditional stores continues to grow.

Measurement and ROE²

When measuring results, there is certainly plenty of data to choose from. The key is to prioritize what to look at, and for what purpose. Individual channel measurement remains important for campaign optimization and content optimization within a particular channel. However, we are placing more emphasis on holistic measures that speak to long-term customer engagement—and that capture *both* the transactional *and* the emotional/experiential relationships formed with consumers. That's a true, more complete measure of business outcomes, one that's in sync with ROE² and its expanded, nontraditional view of marketing and measurement.

Chapter 16

Technology

The Technologies That Empower ROE^2 Are Available, Implementable, and Incredible

Throughout this book, I've touched on many technologies that impact the ability for brands to ignite customer connections. Now we come to a critical area where I'd like to dig into technology more thoroughly. It's a subject that's close to my heart. I've spent the past 30 years helping design and implement technologies that support more and ever more targeted marketing. We live in a time of unprecedented technological advances, which makes a mind-boggling set of powerful tools available to you—with each vendor proclaiming that its technology is the *next big thing*, of course.

Over the next series of technology-related chapters we'll dive more deeply into a framework of the key elements necessary when implementing Return on Experience × Engagement (ROE^2), explore new and topical areas that marketers should understand, and then look at some key lessons learned in implementing these solutions.

What Technologies Enable ROE^2?

Developing a comprehensive guide to all the technologies and approaches that are out in the marketplace is beyond the scope of this book—and would be out of date immediately. There are literally thousands of different technologies that can play a role in ROE². Instead, we'll be drilling into a framework for the key technology enablers of ROE² and some of the business approaches and strategies that make projects succeed. When we discuss technology in the context of igniting customer connections, we can distill the enabling technologies down to the following five capabilities (see Figure 16.1):

1. **Data accumulation, data ingestion, identity management, and data management**—accumulating and linking your data

Figure 16.1 These core elements, no matter what specific solutions you choose, define your marketing infrastructure.

across multiple channels (omnichannel), all in one centralized repository

2. **Analysis**—analyzing and visualizing the wide data sets around customers, content, channels, and brands

3. **Segmentation and targeting**—focusing in on individuals and audiences to deliver relevant and timely content

4. **Content management**—storing discrete pieces of content that can be deployed into a channel or channels

5. **Measurement**—measuring cause and effect of your efforts with these individuals

To implement ROE^2, these five capabilities must be in place, either partially or fully. Let's take a closer look at each.

Data Accumulation and Management

What does data accumulation and linking look like? Data ingestion tools allow you to put structured and unstructured data into a common data store. Linking tools can match customer behavior across postal, e-mail, mobile, mobile apps, web, and more. A flexible data store—most likely based on the Hadoop Distributed File System (HDFS)—permits you to manage, analyze, and add to large sets of data.

While many of the capabilities have been around or practically in place for many years, there has been a revolution of the past two years that is creating game-changing capabilities:

- **Integrated data management.** Today there is little distinction between batch and real-time data management. Common data management technologies can handle both requirements.

- **Early customer connections.** Linking today can include anonymous users and authenticated users, which allows for the ability to connect with customers earlier in their consideration cycle.

- **Seamless data evolution.** Databases can evolve over time without a major redesign in each iteration.

Analysis

The definition of *timely access* has changed as the pace of marketing (and life) accelerates. If you are making real-time decisions based on month-old data, you're not going to be successful, so any analysis capabilities must be as current as possible.

It's also important to differentiate between the general types of analytics:

- *Data science* is a new term that may overlap with business intelligence, but there is a new role emerging today, powered by Big Data, that allows businesspeople who understand the business opportunities and challenges to have easy access to previously uncorrelated sets of data to identify intuitive insights.

- *Real-time decision making* gives you an unprecedented ability to execute strategies like real-time website retargeting if someone abandons a shopping cart, or buy and target media in as little as five milliseconds.

- *Machine learning* includes a broad category of tools that allow you to see deep insights and linkages across diverse sets of data. These approaches use technology to let you uncover the hidden correlations or linkages across the diverse data sets.

Segmentation and Targeting

This capability lets you target individuals (as identified with advanced analytics) with relevant and timely content. In the current, evolving marketing landscape, there are still different tools that enable targeting among the channels. Targeting may happen in your ad tech platform, campaign management system, e-mail platform, or analytical environment—although I expect these to converge over the next few years. But the big opportunity today is to leverage a common data store to drive targeting, and to record and accumulate the results. These sophisticated, powerful, and comprehensive targeting capabilities do not have to be combined in one place to serve your marketing organization well. It's key to focus on implementing some basic capabilities and getting into the market to test them and learn from the process.

Content Management

As we have seen, central to igniting connections and ROE^2 is delivering relevant, impactful, and personalized content to a customer at a point in time. Content management systems (CMSs) have been around for 15 years now, but the recent generation of systems from companies such as Adobe and SiteCore are different in a couple of ways:

- **They can manage the dynamic assembly of content based on a data-driven set of rules.** This capability allows brands to build their content in snippets and then let the technology assemble them in real time.
- **Content can be managed across all of the channels.** This capability helps tremendously with brand consistency and quality.

Content management systems are critical with ROE^2 because, as we saw in our research, experience really drives business outcomes and content is a big part of driving experience. The downside is the need for content creation, and the management of many versions can be expensive and reduce the return on your marketing investments.

Measurement

In the previous chapter, we discussed measurement in some detail; however, it's important to note that measurement is vital to ROE^2, and needs to be considered as part of your technical framework. Without a consistent (across customers, campaigns, and channels) way to evaluate the success of your marketing efforts, you will not be able to push your organization forward. Measurement requires several technology enablers:

- **A clean, consistent data store** that allows you to look back and understand customer dispositions across the elements of engagement and experience over time
- **The capability to attribute business outcomes** to a communication or collection of communications
- **A suite of business intelligence and data visualization tools** that lets you see and distribute the results

A New Development—the Marketing Cloud

The clear risk of publishing a book about a fast-evolving topic like digital marketing is that any discussion of specific technology will be out of date by the time the book is published. However, I believe that one key trend that has emerged and evolved recently will continue to enable better, easier marketing. In the past few years, several companies have launched *marketing clouds*—collections of products (often brought together via company acquisition) that cover some or all of the capabilities just described. (See Figure 16.2.) As marketing clouds mature, some of the complexity and friction will be reduced. However, like all technologies, they are not a panacea.

Marketing Clouds Explored

So what would these capabilities look like when implemented at a small business or an enterprise? The marketing cloud for a small business marketer would be different from the capabilities as implemented at a

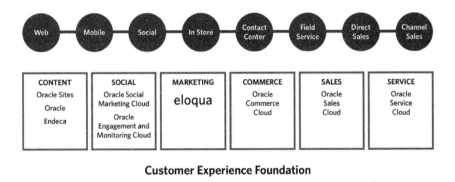

Figure 16.2 Though the specifics will most certainly shift over time, here's an overview of how Oracle defines its marketing cloud.

larger enterprise. But they would serve parallel functions. For example, a small business marketer might combine:

- Constant Contact for e-mail
- HubSpot for website analytics and search engine optimization (SEO)/search engine marketing (SEM)
- Facebook Exchange for targeted social messaging

At a midsize organization or larger enterprise, these capabilities might expand to combine functionality such as:

- Data ingestion tools
- Identity management and linking
- Analytics (online and offline)
- Web tracking
- Campaign management (with multichannel execution)

- Social
- E-mail
- App
- Short message service (SMS)
- Web
- Real-time interaction management
- Loyalty
- Content management
- Attribution and measurement

Vendors that offer marketing clouds for enterprises include IBM, Adobe, Oracle SalesForce, and my company, Epsilon. Each of these has strengths and may fit the needs of your company based on these key questions:

- Do you want to buy, integrate, and run the capabilities yourself, or would you like a partner that provides a more full-service set of capabilities to build, operate, and optimize them?

- Are you focused on identified customers or anonymous customers? Marketing clouds all cover both to a degree, but have a bias in one direction or the other.

- What is your readiness from an identity management, data ingestion, and data management perspective? Some platforms assume the data is ready, whereas others include those capabilities.

Based on your answers to these and other more detailed questions, you will find that marketing clouds offer significant value; however, there is still significant work needed to implement, integrate, and then operate these platforms.

In short, while the capacity and scalability of these capabilities differ, they're largely parallel. Every marketing organization shares the same evolving and expanding needs, and will need to choose the tools appropriate to the scale (and specific needs) of the organization.

Marketing Technology Evolves and Improves

The enabling technologies behind marketing have changed dramatically in a relatively short period of time. Here is a brief look at their evolution.

Phase 1: Disparate Data and Execution Systems (pre-2000)

Prior to 2000, data and execution were generally separated by channels. For example, direct mail required its own database (or some form of data store), process, and supply chain to set up and execute a campaign and measure the impact of direct mail on purchasing. These efforts may have been very specific, such as catalogs driving catalog sales.

The characteristics of this era included limited applications and limits on the amount of data stored (breadth of information as well as history). Data was batch processed, so real-time data in those years seemed like an impossible dream. And this era was marked by static reporting. Think about that green bar computer printout paper for a minute, if you remember it. That was what reporting looked like.

Phase 2: Data Warehousing and Marketing Automation (1998–2012)

At this point, businesses began to implement data warehouses that combined data from different lines of business and different channels. They used this information primarily to

(continued)

execute more sophisticated segmentation, such as identifying multiproduct buyers or customers with high value over an extended period of time. Execution was still driven through separate channels, but there was some coordination in terms of timing and channel(s) selection, such as *We won't mail and call a person with multiple offers on the same day.*

During this era, first-generation marketing automation tools empowered less technical users to set up campaigns. Data was still batch processed, so real-time data had to wait. But on the good side, users could get a comprehensive view of a customer (and all aspects of their relationship) across products, lines of business, and channels. And business intelligence (BI) tools now made it possible for marketers to access reports and to perform some limited analysis.

Phase 3: The Big Data Era (2012–)

In this current phase, we have technology that lets us manage very broad sets of information for marketing. This capability includes information that would be managed in a data warehouse, but extends dramatically beyond traditional data to include web browsing activity, social posts, and e-mail behavioral data. More importantly, this information can be linked and analyzed with added detail and context. For example, *What are the browsing patterns on a smartphone and buying in-store or online?*

Now that individuals spend much of their digital lives traversing various channels, we can identify them through ad networks and target them with unique offers in real time—a capability that would have been impossible back when most digital activity was anonymous. And to make this phase even more marketing-friendly, a wide range of solutions providers now offer marketing clouds that combine applications to manage, execute, and measure campaigns across channels—lowering the financial barrier for entry into this exciting new phase of marketing.

We could devote an entire book to the technology that enables ROE^2. Although such detail is beyond the scope of *Igniting Customer Connections*, our next chapters provide some perspective on the areas that are powerful, current, buzzword-encumbered, and critical to success, including Big Data and advertising technology.

Chapter 17
Big Data

What Do Marketers Need to Know about Big Data?

A few years ago, Big Data existed only in the realm of high-level mathematicians and rarefied areas of business and science. Now Big Data is a key area of marketing technology, one that merits additional discussion and exploration. While entire books have been written on the power and potential of Big Data, here we provide just an overview of five key things that marketers need to know about it.

Big Data Will Help You Create More Relevant Customer Connections

With the rapid evolution of digital technologies, new digital channels, as well as Big Data, marketers can no longer rely on traditional methods of the past to better understand and segment their customers, especially as these customers reach across a broad range of new and somewhat fragmented digital channels.

We all know that these digital consumers move fast when it comes to researching, connecting, and projecting opinion about any brand. They also tend to engage in real-time conversations about their brand experience. As these consumers gain social influence, their opinions (negative or positive) will reach a growing audience that will likely propagate these opinions across more and more channels. All of these interactions and connections result in an increasing amount of Big Data of varying types—including unstructured data, such as a post to a social network.

As consumers embrace an ever-expanding number of digital channels, marketers are now able to use Big Data technologies to significantly expand the number of customer attributes that they can capture and analyze for consideration in their segmentation strategy. This next-generation segmentation approach provides you with an opportunity to produce more personalized and relevant offerings that can directly impact profitable outcomes for your brand.

Working with data scientists as well as new innovations in Big Data technology, businesses are now more easily able to integrate, automate, and take advantage of these very large sets of data from anywhere inside or outside the enterprise for the purposes of capturing additional customer attributes.

These new attributes can include a wide range of structured, semi-structured, and unstructured data. And because Big Data solutions can handle these types of data at a big scale, they easily allow marketers to rapidly build better segments that result in more actionable outcomes for the consumer—and brand.

As advances in Big Data technology evolve, advanced segmentation techniques will also further evolve beyond the ability to capture more attributes about a customer, including propensity to buy, social influence score, and more. Consider the recent evolutions in making data mining technologies simpler and more approachable for mere mortals, as well as the ability to apply predictive analytics technologies on these very large customer data sets. The evolution of these Big Data technologies enables marketers to use these technologies to predict segments that are likely to inspire better experiences for the consumer and more engagement with brands.

Big Data Allows You to Be More Proactive in Delighting and Surprising Your Customers

With the floodgates of real-time consumer conversations wide open on Twitter, Facebook, and Yelp, digitally alert marketers have an opportunity to turn this social data tsunami into actionable information that helps delight and surprise consumers who may have never before engaged with the brand.

Using Big Data to Delight Customers: An Example

Imagine that you're an online seller of car tires. Now imagine Jane, a passionate car owner who frequently engages in conversations about her car on her automaker's most popular forum. Through these conversations, she has developed a huge following of fellow car owners who respect and enjoy her insights.

Jane also notes that she lives in New England and has made it clear that she is having trouble choosing a new set of winter tires for her car. She tells everyone that she has finally narrowed down her selection after researching her options on a consumer recommendation website and online tire shops, as well as with other customers on a wide range of websites, including your online store. The conversation expands with others asking her for her opinion. Jane also just happens to mention your online store as a good place for finding the tires as well as having some "decent deals" these days. She also has been putting videos up on YouTube about her experiences with different tires over the years.

Stepping back from this example, we can see that:

- Jane loves a particular car.
- She has a strong voice in a very large community.
- Her opinion is respected by many.
- She indicates her preferences, her timing (winter tires), and her location.

- She's about to write up her recommendations to a large fan base.
- It seems likely that she'll put up a video.
- She is also a customer of yours.

Now take this example and consider all the folks who are likely to be looking for winter tires from the growing social conversation thread on this subject. You might also find through other data sources that Jane has purchased many tires from your company in the past and just so happens to own a golden retriever named Bentley as noted on her Facebook page. She has also recently opted in to your e-mail list on new tire product announcements.

Understanding and tying all these data sources together in order to surprise and delight Jane with a well-timed offer from your store in the past was quite challenging. However, today, with Big Data technologies that are able to monitor, ingest, integrate, cleanse, and analyze a wide variety of data—including both online and offline data—your store could easily deepen the connection with Jane by generating a timely and very relevant offer for a set of her recommended winter tires. Your intention? To surprise and delight her.

Deepening your data insights would enable you to take things one step further by offering Jane an additional coupon for a dog toy made from recycled tires sourced from your tire recycling partner, and then monitor her response by implementing Big Data social listening solutions to gauge the response. Finally, you may even have the ability to use Big Data predictive analytics technology in order to anticipate Jane's next buying cycle for winter tires.

In the past, the ability to pull all these Big Data sources together was limited and somewhat challenging, primarily because the data solutions of the past weren't built to consider this massive explosion in both social data as well as other channels like video and location information. But now Big Data definitely creates a wealth of new opportunities to deliver positive, memorable, and surprising experiences for your consumers.

Big Data Enables You to Make Better Decisions Faster Than Ever Before

In the past, when marketing professionals had a hunch about their customers, they would call up the data warehouse team in IT and have them gather enough data in a data warehouse (or smaller data mart) to determine if their hunches were valid. The marketer would have to trust that the right data was properly captured, cleansed, transformed, and delivered to the data warehouse in a timely fashion. Such was the world of batch-oriented data warehousing that it wasn't unusual for weeks or maybe even months to pass before an organization was able to perform customer analysis. Average sizes of data warehouses were in the low terabyte range.

A painstaking process was needed to ensure that all the data that was captured was clean, precise, and accurate. The precision of this data was key to performing a valid analysis—though against a much smaller data set than what can be captured and processed today by Big Data platforms, such as Hadoop.

Fast-forward to now, when new Big Data platforms are able to capture much larger sets of varying types of data at higher rates of speed and at a much lower cost to the organization. They can also easily store and process petabytes of data and are available on the cloud, further reducing the cost to organizations by eliminating the requirements for costly IT infrastructure. The cost savings can be significant. Average costs per terabyte for a typical relational database platform run in the range of

$40,000 to $50,000. New Big Data platforms have driven the cost down to as low as $1,000 per terabyte.

As marketers capture more and more data with these Big Data platforms, they face another challenge: how to find the proverbial needle in the haystack of all this marketing data. The good news here is that a new class of highly approachable analysis software, designed to support Big Data, has also emerged.

In order to make the analysis of this Big Data faster for marketing organizations, businesses are employing these new and lower-cost analytic solutions that are more accessible and easier for marketing professionals to use. No longer can marketing organizations wait hours or days for an analysis to be completed by the internal business intelligence teams. Equipped with these new, highly visual analysis solutions, marketers are able to get answers to their hunches themselves and make decisions about their marketing efforts and strategies in much shorter bursts of time than ever before.

The Emerging Internet of Things Will Create Even More Big Data Opportunities

As discussed when exploring channels (Chapter 14), the "Internet of Things" will connect all of us in new and interesting ways. This will also result in a new explosion of data. According to IDC, these devices will generate more than 30 billion autonomously connected end points and $8.9 trillion in revenues by 2020.

With the explosion of connected devices generating a significant amount of Big Data, marketers (working hand in hand with product development) have an opportunity to build new classes of products, as well as enhancements to existing products. The goal? To create even more personalized experiences as well as customer connections than ever before. For example, consider the Vitality Inc. GlowCap—a smart cap that fits on a standard prescription bottle and contains a wireless chip that uses a combination of light and sound to remind consumers to take their prescription medicines. This information is then relayed over the AT&T wireless network. The system can also follow up with the consumer via phone, e-mail, or text, so patients don't miss a dose.

According to Vitality, each time the pill bottle is opened, adherence data is recorded and relayed to Vitality over the AT&T wireless network. This daily adherence information is used to compile periodic progress reports that are sent to patients, caregivers, and doctors, as well as family members. Using a combination of technology innovation as well as wireless capabilities, Vitality is opening up a new opportunity to really engage, connect, and help these consumers.

With this one example, you can see where Big Data comes into play in the context of the Internet of Things, as well as how marketers will need to be in a position to put this Big Data to work on behalf of their consumers—today and into the future.

Marketers Will Need New Skills to Leverage Big Data to Connect Better with Their Customers

According to Gartner Research, Big Data will create more than four million jobs by 2015. Gartner also predicts that businesses will struggle to find skilled Big Data professionals. McKinsey estimates that by 2018, businesses in the United States could face a shortage of at least 150,000 people with deep analytical skills. To continually gather and manage growing Big Data for marketing efforts, companies are already starting to look for marketing pros who also have the skills required to handle the deep analysis of this rising tide of data.

In order to address this growing skill gap—as well as expand the reach of data science skills into other professions—colleges and universities are developing data science programs intended to augment the skills of other professions, including marketing. These universities are also putting together fast-track classes to help address the demands of businesses that are willing to invest in marketing professionals who would benefit from additional expertise in data sciences.

Marketing professionals have been growing their skills in the areas of analytics over the years. But with the explosion of Big Data, the ability to pursue more advanced levels of data science will only serve to benefit them, as well as their businesses and consumers.

Chapter **18**

Online Marketing/ Advertising Technology

What Marketers Need to Know about This Key Area

Any of our technical topics covered here in Part Three could be the subject of a lengthy book. But it would need to be updated daily (or hourly) since technology is an ever-shifting story, driven by new needs and new technologies that meet those needs. Instead, here are five key points about advertising technology (ad tech) that marketers need to know—no matter what you're marketing, how large your organization is, or what your infrastructure looks like.

It's All about the Audience

Most marketers know this instinctively. Marketing is not about an ad or a technology platform. It's about communicating with a living, breathing consumer in a personal and relevant way. Historically, online marketing has not been consumer-focused. Early online advertisers purchased ads on websites using the average profile of visitors to that website as a proxy for targeting. At the time, this approach was better than nothing, but it was based on the flawed assumption that everyone who visited a given site looked the same. New advances in digital media technology now enable marketers to target specific consumers—regardless of which website they visit. This type of media buying, often referred to as *programmatic* or *audience-targeted media*, is growing dramatically.

The Audience Is All about Data

Data is really just a very generic term to describe a marketer's understanding of a consumer. Since online media is all about targeting audiences, you can't accomplish it without data. Historically, the types of data available for use online have been limited at best and seriously flawed at worst. As the types and quality of data available to marketers have evolved, data has become more accurate—and inherently more useful to marketers.

All Data Is Not Created Equal

IP/Geographic Data	Online Behavioral Data	Multisourced Profile Data	Custom Targeting Model
IP Address has 35% chance of being in a geo area with a high concentration of good prospects.	Visited an insurance shopping website. Also visited forbes.com.	User in the 10% of the population most similar to high-value insurance customers based on 20+ verified data sources.	Is in the top 10% of available prospects as determined by a targeting model developed using CRM and third-party data.

$ ⟶ $

Figure 18.1 The complexity, accuracy, and value of data increases as you move from the far left to the far right. While most marketers are still relying on data on the left side of the continuum, more and more marketers (empowered by new capabilities) are taking advantage of better, more accurate data.

Enabling Data for Use Online Requires Technology

Unlike offline marketing, where making data actionable can be as simple as generating a list, using data for digital media requires supporting technologies. This advertising technology ecosystem can vary from marketer to marketer. And there are many technology providers from which to choose. But most brands that are doing a good job of using data in digital media have an ecosystem with the general components shown in Figure 18.2.

Privacy, Privacy, Privacy

As consumers interact with brands and other content online, they usually have the expectation that they are doing so anonymously. This assumption would appear to create challenges for marketers wishing

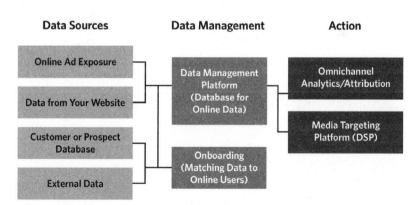

Advertising Technology Ecosystem

Figure 18.2 Here you see the data sources that fuel online marketing, the data management that controls it, and the capabilities (including analytics, attribution, and targeting) that make it more useful the marketers. While the specific elements of your solution will vary, these are the basic components that make digital marketing happen.

to use data to deliver more targeted and relevant messages online. However, in the digital media space, you don't necessarily need to know exactly who someone is in order to deliver a relevant message. The key concept is intelligent anonymity. In other words, marketers can have a lot of intelligence about a consumer without actually knowing who that consumer is. For example, if we use the technology described earlier to match loyalty data to an anonymous cookie, and then gather data on how many times that cookie has visited our website (and how many ads that cookie has seen on other websites), we could wind up with a data set that looks like this:

- Cookie 1289kj
- Visited my website 4 times in past 14 days
- Shopped for men's apparel
- Has 1,000 points on loyalty card
- Spends an average of $900 per year
- Saw my ad on Yahoo! and on XYZ website in past 30 days

Notice that this list does not contain any consumer-identifiable information. That's anonymity with intelligence.

Ultimately, there is very little formal regulation around the use of data in online marketing. However, industry self-regulation groups are building consensus around standard best practices. Most marketers operate somewhere on this continuum:

Bare minimum
- Are fully compliant with all state and federal laws and regulations (e.g., Fair Credit Reporting Act [FCRA], customer proprietary network information [CPNI])

Most major brands
- Comply with industry self-regulation guidelines (Internet Architecture Board [IAB], Direct Marketing Association [DMA])

- Provide consumers with notice of how data is being used, and choice to opt out of targeted advertising

Best-in-class

- Do not permanently associate personally identifiable information (PII) with a cookie

- Do not include uniquely identifiable information on a cookie

- Make sure that consumer identification data never leaves client's secure environment

A great tool for enabling best-in-class online privacy is the AdChoices platform, developed and sanctioned by a consortium of industry groups and brands. See the AdChoices site at www .youradchoices.com for more information.

Don't Forget the Power of People

Much of the discussion about advances in digital media focuses on data and technology. But brands cannot be successful by concentrating on just these two components. The most common concern I hear from brands looking to be more successful online is: *I just can't find enough good people.* You need great people to help you be successful in this space. The need for human brainpower is particularly acute in a few key areas—navigating the complex online ecosystem, performing day-to-day management, and ensuring alignment.

- **Navigating the complex online ecosystem.** For years, the industry has been expecting consolidation and simplification in the online advertising ecosystem. But there are still hundreds (or thousands) of advertising technology companies serving various roles in this space. And the creation of new innovative start-ups continues to outpace the rate of consolidation. So it's unlikely that complexity will go away anytime soon. To create an ecosystem that works for your brand, you need people who have a deep understanding of online advertising technology and how the pieces fit together.

- **Day-to-day management of data-driven media programs.** Teams that have spent their careers doing traditional media buying are often not equipped with the analytic skills and other capabilities necessary for this new data-driven media world.

- **Achieving true omnidata for omnichannel.** Internal brand organization alignment is also essential. As the barriers between online marketing and direct marketing begin to crumble, marketing organizations will need to wrestle with incentive structures and delivery models that hinder a true *omnidata for omnichannel* approach.

Chapter 19
Putting Technology to Work

Strategies for Implementing ROE^2 Technology Successfully

T he number of technological options available can be overwhelming. To simplify the process, I want to provide some key strategies that can help your marketing organization overcome the main challenges raised when implementing the technology that enables Return on Experience × Engagement (ROE^2).

Create a Partnership between Information Technology and Marketing

This relationship has historically been adversarial. Marketing has often been at the bottom of information technology (IT)'s priorities, so much of the technology work was outsourced. However, because of the breadth of impact and real-time nature of today's next-generation marketing technologies, *IT must be involved*, and must remain an active participant. How the work gets done may still be a combination of internal and external resources, but there has to be IT involvement and a common strategy.

Develop a Consistent Master Data Management Strategy

With the ever-increasing amount of data under management in marketing systems, it's critical that there be a shared view and definition of what the data means across the enterprise. In a perfect world, a piece of data would exist in only one place. But today the reality is that one piece of data will be managed in many places. If different parts of your organization are allowed to have their own definitions, then chaos will erupt during data analysis. So take a broad, consistent view of data management, one that ensures integrity, consistency, and order. Getting data management right from the start is even more important as every organization struggles with ever-increasing volumes of data.

Know That Implementing Technology Is Always Harder Than It Seems

When implementing ROE², it's important to make incremental steps and not be daunted by the inherent complexity that comes with increasing your marketing capabilities exponentially. One of the benefits of today's technologies and more agile implementation methodologies is that they allow for a series of smaller, more incremental deliverables. This approach is the opposite of older technologies and approaches that needed to be planned months, or sometimes years, in advance. Today, projects can have a small scope at the beginning and be extended in a series of smaller deliverables. Marketing and IT professionals work side by side to define, build, and test new features or capabilities.

This approach benefits your organization in two key ways. First, it lets you get some functionality faster and start driving business value. And second, it lowers the risk of a specific project by enabling you to learn about the capabilities and technologies as you go, making changes based on firsthand experience.

Beware of Bright, Shiny Solutions

If a technology seems too good to be true, it is. There are no magic bullets. If a partner or vendor promises that its wonderful solution will manage all of your data seamlessly and optimize your interactions automatically, it is not being truthful. Yes, there are incredible tools out there, and new ones emerging regularly. But you must take a deliberate approach and select the right combination of capabilities—and then implement them in a pragmatic manner.

Find the Right Starting Point

Where to start the journey to enable you company is dependent on your own situation, but here are a few guidelines that may be helpful:

- **Start where the money is.** One piece of advice I always give to companies that are looking at planning for new technologies is to begin where those technologies can have the biggest business impact. If there is a channel or a segment of customers or a product that represents risk or opportunity—start there. Deconstruct your business problem down to the true root causes, develop a hypothesis on what you could do to overcome the causes of your problem, and then link that hypothesis to a technical solution. Never start with a technology looking for a business problem to solve.

- **Start simple and evolve.** If you are not in the market getting results and learning in a few months, it is taking too long. Even if the first phase seems ridiculously simple, do that. You not only will learn about the technology but will also get marketing learnings that will inform the scope of the next phase.

- **If it's not working, kill it fast.** If you try a new technology and you don't see that value after a few iterations, stop and move on. Many of these solutions can be procured in an *on-demand* model that limits or reduces up-front costs.

Technology Enables, but It Isn't Everything

In an era when tech start-ups dominate the business world and new capabilities make marketing faster, more targeted, and smarter, I'd like to conclude with what seems like a counterintuitive point. Technology isn't the salvation of marketing. No amount of technology can match the time-tested smarts of an experienced marketer, a powerful executive vision, and the commitment of the entire marketing team—not to mention exceptional products and/or services. While technology may accelerate and enable the brain of your organization, people remain at its heart. Giving your marketing team the right set of capabilities, such as ROE², helps your organization—no matter how small or large, or what market segment—achieve its goals, now and far into the future.

Chapter 20
Consumer Privacy

Address This Critical Issue with Transparency, Knowledge, Respect, and Responsibility

Customer connections, atomic moments of truth, deeper engagement, and a better experience—all of the ideas and strategies we've explored so far are based on connecting with customers more closely. The many benefits this closer connection brings to your business and the consumer are clear—from more relevant messaging and offers to greater efficiency to better results. But when citizens and consumers become valued customers and prospects, it also raises a key issue—privacy. Here we highlight the importance of respecting customer privacy, and share some of the ground rules that help ensure it.

Why Is Privacy an Issue?

The digital era enables businesses to compile, share, analyze, use, and store more data than ever before—more easily, and at a lower cost. The growing volume of highly detailed data has triggered an ongoing privacy debate. It's a major topic of discussion—not just within the marketing community, but around the dinner table, in the news, and on Capitol Hill. Any marketing organization that ignores its customers' privacy does so at its own peril.

As we established earlier, businesses operate differently than in the distant past of a decade ago—they move faster and rely on more channels to connect to their customers. To meet the fast-evolving, diverse needs of their customers, they're gathering more data, creating privacy concerns that never existed back when consumer data was collected by an actual person and processed by hand.

Here are just some of the reasons why consumer privacy is such a hot topic:

- **Consumer data is increasing exponentially and getting more detailed.** Any business that wants to target its customers more accurately can collect remarkably detailed data on offline and online shopping habits, social media activity, and much more. The amount of data that is now available about consumers is remarkable and ever-increasing, thanks to digital channels that manufacture massive amounts of information about what we look at, how we feel, where we are, and what our intent may be. How marketers use this data to determine offers and communication strategies raises issues around what level of differentiated offer is appropriate for each consumer.

- **The cost of data gathering has never been lower.** The ability to gather, store, and analyze large volumes of consumer data used to be limited to organizations that had the deep pockets necessary to pay for expensive databases, storage, analytics, and other premium technologies. Now these capabilities are within reach of almost any business.

- **Consumers are more aware.** A consumer shopping for a pair of shoes online finds that unrelated websites are displaying ads for the same shoes. *How did that happen?* The invisible and often mysterious workings of cookies and other behavioral tracking technologies are becoming more apparent to consumers. To ease potential issues and allay fears, marketing organizations need to educate consumers on their practices—and protect privacy at all levels.

- **Privacy protections are evolving.** As technology advances, consumer awareness, media attention, and legislative and regulatory attention have increased in parallel. Privacy standards are evolving within our industry through self-regulation—and privacy protections are strengthening through state and federal regulation. The fluid nature of the issue merits attention and focus from marketing professionals at all levels, in all industries.

Why Gather Data?

It's important to remember the underlying reasons why businesses gather consumer data. By using this data, you can deliver more relevant content about goods and services that consumers actually care about versus blind mass marketing that fails to reach the right audience. By knowing preferences, you can provide a better customer experience, encourage deeper engagement, and lower marketing costs by creating more customer value—at its core, a mutually beneficial relationship.

What Should Your Company Be Doing?

There is an ever-changing balance between consumer privacy and technological innovation—one that needs to be respected and maintained. Four key qualities (shown in Figure 20.1) can help guide your organization through the evolving world of consumer privacy—transparency, respect, knowledge, and responsible use:

1. **Transparency** in how you gather, use, store, and share data

2. **Respect** for your customers

3. **Knowledge** of consumer privacy

4. **Responsible use** of information

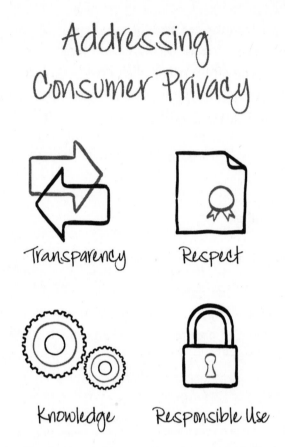

Figure 20.1   Transparency, Respect, Knowledge, and Responsible Use.

Transparency: For the Good of Your Company and Our Industry

Transparency is the key to getting customers to trust your brand. Transparency means:

- **Going public.** Post your privacy policy publicly on your website or by providing a method for consumers to easily access this information.

- **Being clear.** Explain how you are using data through robust privacy statements in your privacy policy.

- **Make it easy.** Provide consumers an easy way to access, amend, or delete their data. And provide an easy method to opt out with a clear description of practical implications of opting out.

- **Respect your customers.** Convey a high level of respect to customers in all policies, communications, and interactions.

For example, at Epsilon we provide extensive information on our website to educate the public about our business and how direct marketing works. Beyond our privacy policy, we help consumers understand the marketing industry. Our website includes a Consumer Knowledge Center, complete with a guide to direct marketing, glossary of terms, and FAQs. We also have a mechanism for consumers to request information about the data we have on them and multiple options for opting out of our services in our Consumer Preference Center.

Why do we do this? Because transparency is important to our customers—and to our business. Just like it is to yours.

Respect: For Your Customers

Privacy is about respecting the consumers' information and their right to determine how it should be used. When you start with that principle, respect helps ensure that you don't take actions that violate consumer privacy in an unethical way. Respecting data includes:

- **Playing by the rules.** Follow industry standards, and adhere to any applicable laws that provide data protections.

- **Revisiting your privacy promises.** Stay up-to-date as you design and build new products and services.

- **Taking additional precautions.** Handle sensitive information, such as financial or health information, with even more attention to privacy.

- **Securing information.** Stay in line with industry best practices, and train employees on proper data handling procedures.

Most important, remember to honor the promises made in your privacy policy. As you build respect with your customers and become a trusted brand, you will find a deeper engagement with those customers—the kind of engagement that demands respect for privacy.

Knowledge: For Your Company

Everyone in marketing needs to think about consumer privacy. But more importantly, they need to educate themselves on privacy issues, especially emerging issues, to stay up to date on the latest trends and news. More organizations are bringing on chief privacy officers (CPOs) for just such a purpose—to stay in touch with all of the evolving details related to privacy, and to advocate for fair use of data. But even without a CPO, your organization can take steps to stay current on privacy issues. Joining an organization such as the Direct Marketing Association (www.thedma.org) gives you instant access to extensive information and resources related to consumer privacy—including data-driven marketing best practices. Engage in the dialogue at a national, regional, or local level. But definitely engage.

Responsibility: For Security and More

Consumer privacy also means considering security concerns. We've all heard the numerous stories of security breaches large and small that put organizations in the news. In fact, even Epsilon was impacted by a security incident back in April 2011. And we learned a lot from that experience. No company is immune in today's digital ecosystem, so it's important to remain diligent and committed to protecting customer data and putting all available measures in place. Marketers should answer these key questions:

- What consumer data do you really need?
- What purposes are you using it for?

- Have you disclosed these uses?
- How long do you need to retain that data?
- How do you (or a third party) store it?
- How do you protect it?
- Do you supply it to third parties?
- If so, how do *they* use and store it?
- How do you monitor outside use of your data?

Asking these questions can help you safeguard the consumer data and keep the promises you made to your customers. These are just some of the many questions raised by the complex issue of consumer privacy. In general, the rule of thumb is to gather only information that you intend to use. But even that data carries a significant responsibility.

I Am Andy Frawley's Data

At Epsilon, we provide an extensive section of information for consumers on our website to increase transparency and educate consumers (www.epsilon.com/consumer-info). After all, consumer data is the lifeblood of our work, and we have to let consumers know that we respect their data and, more important, give them the option to see their data and opt out if they choose. I took a closer look at my own data recently by submitting my own information. (See Figure 20.2.)

In addition to the basics (my name, age, address, household details, etc.), there were also listings of the main categories of my recent purchases—including apparel and accessories, home office supplies and electronics, and sports and hobbies. Was I surprised at the data or disturbed at the level of detail? No. And if I were, it's clear how I could opt out.

(continued)

Marketing Data Summary

Thank you for your recent inquiry to Epsilon. Your privacy is very important to us and we want to provide you with a clear understanding of the type of information that may be contained in our marketing databases. The information is used by companies and nonprofit organizations to provide you with offers that may be relevant and of interest to you.

Household Demographic, Lifestyle Interests, and Real Property Information

Epsilon gathers household-level demographic, lifestyle interests, and real property information from a variety of sources, which include public records (such as property deeds and telephone directories) and proprietary sources (entities with which Epsilon has an agreement to receive certain data). These sources of information help Epsilon clients to further understand a household's interests. For example, a household interested in supporting charitable causes may receive a mailing from a local charity asking for donations to the upcoming clothing drive.

What you see below are the types of data that Epsilon may have about any given household. Your specific data includes the following:

Household Data

Last Name	FRAWLEY
First Name	ANDREW
Address	
City	
State	
Zip	
Phone Number	
Do Not Call Flag	YES

Household Demographics

Approximate Age	51 to 52
Approximate Ages of Others in the Household	45 to 54
Presence of Children	Yes

Self Reported Information

Epsilon Shoppers Voice® sends surveys to households in the United States and Canada to obtain information on consumer opinions and shopping behavior. The survey asks questions about the products that a household buys or uses and general household interests. When consumers voluntarily answers these questions, Epsilon gathers information about the responses, to better understand a household. If Epsilon has received a Shoppers Voice survey from your household, a copy of that survey is enclosed.

Figure 20.2   Marketing Data Summary.

Household Purchases

Epsilon's Household Purchase Database contains consumer names and addresses, along with generalized household purchase information, to help understand the types of purchases people have made. Your data includes the following:

Most Recent Purchase Date Range	0-12 Months
Purchases in the Following Categories	Apparel and Accessories
	Women's Apparel and Accessories
	Men's Apparel and Accessories
	Jewelry
	Children's Merchandise
	Food
	Media: Books, Music, Magazines, and Newsletters
	Business Merchandise
	Garden and Outdoor
	Home and Gifts
	Home Office and Electronics
	Sports and Hobbies

The information that you have received as part of this Marketing Data Summary is used to create groups of consumers who may be interested in similar types of marketing messages. Not all of the information described below is collected; much of it is based on educated guesses about what your household may look like. The information below is used at a general level to send more targeted advertising but it does not describe your household specifically.

Group D

Average Household Income:	$182,047
Homeowner:	Highly likely
Average Age of Head of Household:	50
Average Length of Residence:	16 years
Percentage with Kids:	73% (above average)
Education Level:	Highly educated, likely college or graduate level
Favorite Channels:	Mail, online, retail
Profession:	Executive
Credit Card User:	Yes
Auto Ownership:	Luxury vehicles
Discretionary Spending:	Children's merchandise, sports apparel, home furnishings, and magazines

Interests: Donating to charitable causes, investing, gourmet food, wines, fitness, golfing, running/jogging, walking for health, hiking, cycling, domestic traveling, cruises, crafts, boating, sailing, and photography.

Figure 20.2 *(continued)*

The foundation of all data-driven marketing is data, of course. How you treat that data is of the utmost importance. After all, in a consumer-empowered world, the consumer controls the flow of data. And without consumer data, none of the results discussed in the earlier chapters of *Igniting Customer Connections* would have ever happened. The spark would simply go out.

Consider the consumer your partner. Think of every consumer as a long-term customer. Put yourself in customers' shoes. Make decisions about their data as if it were your own, because your data is out there somewhere, too. I know it—I've just seen mine.

Stay True to Your Principles

Consistency is important when addressing consumer privacy issues. It's important to take a stand and stick with it. At Epsilon, we have remained steadfast to three principles:

1. **Consumers should have transparency and choice.** Epsilon was one of the first companies to give consumers access to the information we maintain by offering a marketing data summary, such as the one I obtained with my data information. We also provide a way for consumers to manage their opt-out preferences through our online Consumer Preference Center.

2. **Marketing data should be used for marketing purposes only.** The data that Epsilon maintains is used to deliver an offer or information to consumers who might be interested in one of our clients' products or services. The vast majority of customers of our clients have opted in to receive communications, and they can opt out at any time.

3. **Companies have an obligation to use data responsibly.** We are stewards of our clients' information, and we take that responsibility

very seriously. We never allow our data to be used for nonmarketing activities, such as granting credit, conducting employment background checks, or obtaining health insurance, and we strongly support corrective action when marketing data is used for any purpose other than marketing.

Creating your own clear set of principles and making them public is an important step. While many marketing organizations (and their partners) say they respect consumer privacy, nothing beats putting it in writing—and spreading the word.

Chapter 21
A Few Final Words on ROE^2

Before You Start Igniting *Your* Customer Connections

One of the great things about writing *Igniting Customer Connections* was watching the concept of Return on Experience × Engagement (ROE^2) come into sharper and sharper focus. With every meeting where our team discussed and defined ROE^2, every research project we completed, each conversation with a marketing executive—the underlying *rightness* and power of ROE^2 became more and more apparent.

From years of working with clients, I knew the importance of experience and engagement. I knew that many brands were not giving these areas the attention they deserved. And I knew that investing in these areas delivered real returns in terms of building brand and business equity. But here at the end of this book, I know, with data to back it up, that Return on Experience × Engagement—ROE^2—is real. And you do, too. It gives you a powerful tool to determine where to invest your marketing spend. And it's a more accurate measurement of marketing results than traditional return on investment (ROI). More importantly,

ROE^2 gives you a new way to create, nurture, and *ignite* your customer connections.

The most exciting part of this book happens after it's over, when you take the insights and advice and make them part of your work. I appreciate the opportunity to pass along these concepts—and I look forward to hearing about the impressive and exciting results you're able to achieve with them.

ACKNOWLEDGMENTS

I could never have attempted to write this book without the help of some of my amazing associates at Epsilon. I am always amazed and inspired by the blend of creativity and science that they can bring to any opportunity. While many associates helped form these ideas, I would like to specifically thank the following people who provided their time to conduct the research, contribute content, fact-check information, and spread the word about *Igniting Customer Connections*:

Paula Ausick, John Bartold, Stephen Bernstein, Kim Bramante, Diane Bruno, Anna Cherkasky, Kristine Cieri, Kim Finnerty, Jeanette Fitzgerald, Gaylord Garraway, Taleen Ghazarian, Deirdre Heisler, John Immesoete, George Israel, Chuck Jiang, Bryan Kennedy, Cathy Lang, Kevin Mabley, Gillian MacPherson, Jade Mangahis, Andrew McKellar, Kerry Morris, Jessica Nable, Brian Peterson, Elizabeth Phillibert, Karen Phillips, Vic Piano, Tim Prunk, Kris Shahinian, Michael Shur, Liz Soto, Irene Stavisky, Nicole Tachibana, Wayne Townsend, Suzie Weaver, Andy Wilder, John Young, and Bob Zurek.

I also have the unique opportunity to work with some of the most brilliant marketing minds in the world—my clients. Again, many clients over the years helped formed the thinking in this book. But I would specifically like to thank Pat Brady, Elmer Smith, and John Costello, who agreed to be interviewed for the book.

Others who provided valuable input to the process of writing a book included Bryan Person, Jay Baer, Jeff Hayzlett, and Chris DeFrancesco (illustrations).

With a busy schedule, I wrote this book on airplanes and nights and weekends. I would like to thank my wife Juli for her ongoing patience and encouragement over the past six months. I would also like to thank my children—Sam, Erica, and J.P.—for their perspectives and opinions on social media and how it is influencing experience and engagement with the younger generation.

Thanks to Richard Narramore and Tiffany Colon at John Wiley & Sons for their input on structuring and shaping this book, and Deborah Schindlar for coordinating its design and production.

Finally, I would like to thank my editor, Stona Fitch. Without his guidance, insight, and patience, this project would never have reached a conclusion. He has been a pleasure to work with.

ABOUT THE AUTHOR

Andy Frawley is President of Epsilon Data Management, LLC, a global leader in creating customer connections that build brand and business equity. He has 30 years of operating experience, including 25 years at the senior management level, within agency, marketing services, consulting, enterprise software, software as a service (SaaS), and professional services companies. He's also a leading subject matter expert on digital marketing, including e-mail marketing, customer relationship management (CRM), Big Data, database marketing, marketing automation, and customer value management.

He joined Epsilon (a division of Alliance Data) in 2009 to lead digital marketing, and quickly became president in 2012. Epsilon is a new breed of marketing company for a consumer-empowered world. Its unique approach harnesses the power of rich data, world-leading technologies, engaging creativity, and transformative ideas to ignite connections between brand and customers—delivering dramatic results.

This book distills Epsilon's learnings—gleaned from working with some of the world's leading marketers and from its more than 5,000 associates—into actionable strategies that you can use in your marketing, whether you're a start-up or a major international brand. It provides insights from original consumer research and analysis of hundreds of thousands of data points gathered from leading brands, combined with petabytes of third-party and first-party data, that are pushing the boundaries of marketing.

INDEX